Standardized Testing

Susan Abbott, M.A.

Teacher Created Materials, Inc.

Cover Design by Darlene Spivak

Made in U.S.A.

ISBN 1-57690-124-6

Order Number TCM 124

Table of Contents

Introduction

Throughout my teaching career, I have been profoundly motivated by the desire to ensure that every student receives an education that is equitable and fair, especially in the opportunities that education provides for success. Unfortunately, I have witnessed many inequities in the standardized testing practices of schools and districts. I have seen students defeated, denied access to programs, and prevented from reaching for goals, all because of a single standardized test score. The motivation and hopes that underlie this book include the following:

> Teachers and administrators must become more knowledgeable about standardized testing principles, practices, uses, and abuses.

> Teachers must raise a collective voice to ensure that standardized test scores are used appropriately and only in the best interest of students.

> Teachers must utilize innovative ways to integrate test practice with curriculum to prepare students for mandated standardized testing.

> Teachers must present a strong case for authentic assessment as a partner for standardized testing to ensure that a student's achievement is evaluated on an ongoing basis by what the student can do, not what the student cannot or did not do.

When I think about the call for a national test to measure student achievement, *Leo the Late Bloomer*, a wonderful book by Robert Kraus, comes to mind. The story tells of Leo who just can't read, write, or speak, until one day, "in his own good time," he blooms. His first words are, "I made it!"

Like Leo, students can and will make it if they have time, help, and opportunities for success. Students should never be tracked, labeled, or denied access because of standardized test scores. Standardized tests do not improve the quality of education; good schools and good teachers do!

Standardized Testing: An Overview

History

During the late 1970s and early 1980s, standardized testing was heavily criticized, and a vigorous debate took place about its negative effects on students. Support began to build for authentic assessment practices that allowed student progress to be measured by continuous, multifaceted strategies rather than a single test score.

However, after the publication of *A Nation at Risk* in 1983, accountability once again came to the forefront. Testing programs expanded greatly, and results were widely publicized. As programs for school improvement proliferated in the 1980s, the trend to assess the quality of schools and teachers by using standardized tests also grew in influence (Ryan & Cooper, 1995, p. 256). There was a public outcry demanding better educational quality. Teachers responded by criticizing the tests: they put forth a plea for authentic measures, performance-based measures that would focus on the student's work to determine achievement. In an effort to make standardized testing practices more authentic, achievement tests were produced that called for written responses reflecting how an answer was obtained. These met with limited success, with perhaps the most dismal failure occurring in California with the California Learning Assessment System *(CLAS)*. Content and scoring procedures infuriated parents and students, leading to picketing and student walkouts. The test was abandoned, but the idea remains that writing ability, reasoning, critical thinking, and process are important considerations in standardized measurement. Slowly, publishers are making efforts to incorporate these into standardized tests.

Teachers responded by criticizing the tests: they put forth a plea for authentic measures, performance-based measures that would focus on the student's work to determine achievement.

1

Currently, widespread reports of the poor achievement of American children in a globally competitive society have raised concerns for educational standards and standardized tests to prove content mastery. There is a strong movement in the United States to create national standards for student achievement linked to some form of national assessment (Ryan & Cooper, 1995, p. 256).

Can a child's intelligence, academic competence, and potential for success be adequately measured by a standardized test? No. To believe so would go against the grain of what we know as educators: each child is unique; each has strengths; each has talent to develop. Will standardized testing continue? Yes, if history and current trends are any indication. More and more policymakers believe that student achievement will increase with high standards and that the attainment of these standards can be measured by a standardized test. Consequently, it is vital that teachers understand the language, practices, procedures, limitations, and cautions of standardized testing.

> **Can a child's intelligence, academic competence, and potential for success adequately be measured by a standardized test? No.**

What Is Standardized Testing?

As early as 1845 Horace Mann suggested administrating tests with large numbers of questions and the standardization of answers (Ryan, 1994, p. 3). A test is called "standardized" for several reasons: there is a *standard* set of questions that every student answers; there is a *standard* procedure for administering the questions that must be strictly adhered to; there is a set of norms based upon the *standard* responses of a sample group; finally, it provides a *standard* for comparison. Standardization makes it possible to generalize and to draw conclusions about the data and their implications (Sanders & Horn, 1995).

The purposes and uses of standardized tests are multiple and varied. Standardized tests are often mandated at the local, state, and national levels. Comparisons are widely publicized, ranking schools within a district and county as well as across states and the nation. Results are commonly used for funding decisions and hiring practices. Standardized tests can measure a single skill such as reading, or they can be multiple-skill batteries. "Most of the achievement tests administered by school districts are test batteries that include sections on reading, writing, language, mathematics concepts, mathematics computation, social studies, and science" (Ruddell, 1997, p. 279). Most are norm-referenced devices, but standards-based educational reform may lead to a wider use of criterion-referenced instruments.

Test Your Knowledge of Standardized Testing

Standardized testing is an issue that evokes heated debate, strong opinions, and a wide range of emotional outbursts from the public as well as the educational community. It is a complex topic easily misunderstood and often fraught with misconceptions. The statements below form the basis of this book. Test yourself before going on to the next chapter, and discover the facts, assumptions, and misconceptions that underlie standardized testing! Is each statement true or false?

_____ 1. The basic purpose of standardized testing is to compare groups of children or to compare individual performances to that of a group.

_____ 2. Extreme scores (those that are very high or very low) are the least reliable and require additional measures to verify.

_____ 3. When using a standardized test, you can assume it is both reliable and valid.

_____ 4. The most valid score on a standardized test is the raw score.

_____ 5. Every student is capable of working at the median level of the national norms.

_____ 6. You can accurately measure a teacher's instructional ability by examining the test scores of his or her students.

_____ 7. Standardized tests are excellent predictors of later accomplishments.

_____ 8. Objective scoring implies "fair" or justifiable scoring.

_____ 9. A power test is intended to measure what a student knows, not how fast that student can work.

_____ 10. The total, comprehensive score, not the subtest scores, provides the most useful information about a student's performance.

_____ 11. If a student receives a score equivalent to the 55th percentile, that student has answered 55% of the questions correctly.

_____ 12. It is not ethical for teachers to "teach to the test."

Standardized testing is an issue that evokes heated debate, strong opinions, and a wide range of emotional outbursts from the public as well as the educational community.

3

Whether or not these statements are true or false can be discovered by reading through the pages of this Professional's Guide. More important than the answers, though, will be the reasoning, widespread misconceptions, and educational implications that accompany them. An understanding of these can facilitate educators in making wise, student-friendly use of standardized test data as just one part of a multidimensional system of assessment.

Concluding Remarks

"Research evidence from the past two decades documents the fact that testing policies have not had the positive effects intended, while they have had unintended negative consequences for the quality of American schooling and for the equitable allocation of school opportunities" (Lieberman, 1991, p. 220).

In a quest to improve educational assessment, "states have first instituted and then dropped or redirected assessment procedures with names like basic competencies, mastery learning, criterion-referenced testing, and, more recently, holistic, authentic, outcomes-based, and performance-based assessment" (Manzo, 1997, p. 35). Currently, criticism about the educational achievement of our nation's young people is abundant. There is a thrust for accountability, perhaps a symptom of "millennium fever," that has policymakers shouting for national standards and national assessments. Standardized testing is once again in the limelight, and it is imperative that teachers understand its practices, limitations, and implications.

There is a thrust for accountability, perhaps a symptom of "millennium fever," that has policymakers shouting for national standards and national assessments.

4

The Vocabulary of Standardized Testing

Conceptual Foundation

It is important to have a clear understanding of the terminology of standardized testing. Many score interpretation problems stem from the misuse of terms or misconceptions about their true meanings. As professionals, teachers must have a theoretical foundation before they begin interpreting scores and using those interpretations for academic decisions. Study the terms carefully; read, analyze, and synthesize the content of this section. Student access and success may well depend on your careful scrutiny of these concepts.

Statistical Terms

- **Reliability** is consistency. How consistent is the test in measuring what it says it measures? Is it accurate? Is it stable from one testing period to the next? How much confidence does the score elicit (is it true or real)? Can it be believed? This is especially important when a standardized test is used as a pre/post measure of achievement. Reliability for alternate forms of the same test (Forms A and B, G and H, etc.) is crucial when program or teacher accountability is being measured.

- **Validity** means that the test measures what it says it measures. Probably the most important facet of this is *content validity,* the extent to which the test content is similar to the curriculum. No test should be used unless the administration and faculty read it carefully for content validity. In practice, though, this is seldom a reality; in fact, the test content is often a secret,

> As professionals, teachers must have a theoretical foundation before they begin interpreting scores and using those interpretations for academic decisions.

5

kept hidden until test day. *Predictive validity* is also an important aspect to consider. When the test is used for selection purposes, for example, placement in a gifted or accelerated program, the test must be related to success in that program.

- **Raw score** is the number correct. This is the only true or real score. It is not extrapolated from another score. It is not based on the standard responses of a sample population. It is a fact.
- **Mean** is the average score of a group. Add the raw scores of each participant and divide by the number of participants. The mean is a mathematical average, so half of the students must fall below it, and half will score above.
- **Median** is the middle score. Median will be the same as the mean. Half of the students score higher, half lower. It is the score that falls at the 50th percentile. Often, policymakers decry the educational system, saying every child should achieve at the national average. It is a mathematical impossibility for every child to score at or above the mean or median.
- **Mode** is the most frequently occurring score.

It is a mathematical impossibility for every child to score at or above the mean or median.

Study this group of nine students and the raw scores they received on the comprehension section of the Gates-MacGinite standardized reading test:

Student	Raw Score	
Susie M.	40	
Joelle A.	41	
Julie D.	33	
Jonisha C.	32	
Thaun X.	**30**	Mean (Mathematical Average) Median (Middle Score)
Hector R.	**26**	Mode (Most Frequent Score)
Robert E.	26	Mode
Juan M.	26	Mode
Mary E.	16	

- **Converted score** is the name given to types of scores that have been derived from the raw scores of the norm-referenced sample. It is a score that has been extrapolated; in other words, it has been interpreted from the raw scores. All scores (percentiles, stanines, grade equivalents, etc.) **except the raw scores**, are converted scores.
- **Standard score** is a converted score assigned by the test publisher to each raw score. It allows for comparisons of alternate forms of a test. Probably the best example is the *Scholastic Aptitude Test*. Raw scores are converted to numbers such as

480, 520, and so forth; these are standard scores that represent the placement value of a raw score across varied forms of the test. The standard score does not show a position within a group of 100 scores. Rather, it helps interpret a score from one form of the test (e.g., Form A) to that of an alternate form (e.g., Form B).

- **Percentile** is a converted score that shows the position of a score within 100 scores. For example, a score at the 55th percentile means that the student scored equal to or above 55% of the students in the norm-referencing group. Be careful! A percentile score is not the same thing as percent correct!

- **Stanine** is a combination of the terms "standard" and "nine." Also a converted score, it provides another way of comparing scores in a norm-referencing group; generally, it is best used when making group comparisons. The following grid shows the relationship of percentile and stanine rankings as well as commonly accepted achievement rankings for each level.

> Grade equivalent is the most estimated, and the least reliable of all scores.

Percentile/Stanine/Achievement Ranking Grid

Percentile	Stanine	Achievement Ranking
Below 4 %tile	1	Well Below Average
5 — 11 %tile	2	Below Average
12 — 23 %tile	3	
24 — 40 %tile	4	Low Average
41 — 60 %tile	5	Average
61 — 77 %tile	6	High Average
78 — 89 %tile	7	Above Average
90 — 96 %tile	8	
Above 97 %tile	9	Superior

- **Grade equivalent** is the most estimated and the least reliable of all scores. It is the estimate of an estimate. It is a mathematical interpolation. A grade equivalent is expressed in terms of year/month; for example, a grade equivalent of 4.6 represents fourth grade, sixth month. It expresses a grade level for which the raw score is the estimated average. It does not mean that a student is reading or doing math or spelling at that grade level; rather, on this test the student performed equivalently to those in a particular grade. "Grade equivalent scores are intended to indicate the average level of performance for students in each month of each grade" (Weirsma & Jurs, 1990, p. 127).

These are popular scores, often demanded by administrators and parents, but the least reliable and most misconstrued of any scores. They are most damaging to self-esteem. The International Reading Association has taken a firm position against the use of grade equivalent scores.

- **Norm-reference group** is commonly called the sample population. This is the population that sampled or tried the test. From the scores of this sample population, the performance of individuals is separated so that there is a distribution of scores. Norm-referenced tests are standardized on groups of individuals, and typical performances for students of certain ages or in certain grades are obtained. Perhaps the most important point to remember about the norm-referenced group is that of bias. Any student who takes a particular standardized test is scored through comparison to this norm-referenced group. If the population of the norm-referenced group does not match the population of the group being compared, the potential for bias is great.

- **Standard error or measurement (SEM)** is a powerful, yet little known, concept. Unlike percentiles, stanines, and standard scores, SEM is seldom listed in the manual that accompanies the tests a teacher must administer. To get the standard error of a test, a technical manual or call to the publisher is often necessary. The SEM "is a statistic that provides an estimate of the possible magnitude of error present in an obtained score; it is the amount by which the student's obtained score may differ from his or her hypothetical true score due to errors of measurement" (Ruddell, 1997, p. 232). In other words, it is the "plus or minus" estimate of test error. On any day, on that particular test, the student's real, true score could be plus or minus either a number of points or a number of months. Either way, consequences can be devastating.

> *Scenario:* A local high school district uses a standardized reading test to measure reading skills of all incoming middle/junior high school students; they are tested in the last month of their eighth grade year (grade level 8.9). Based on the score each student receives, a high school placement is made in either a remedial, regular, or college preparatory English class. The guidelines for placement require that students be reading at grade level or above or they cannot be placed in the college prep course. Notices are sent home advising parents and students of placement. An eighth grade student who gets a placement of 8.6, 8.7, or 8.8 is informed that he or she must take regular English, not the college prep class.

What is wrong with this? The standard error of the test in question is + or - (plus or minus) .3 (three months). The test maker is acknowledging that the score could well be three months higher or lower just because of error inherent in testing. Yet, a possible life altering decision has been made for those students because the SEM was not part of the placement equation.

Think, also, about the effect this can have on program or teacher accountability. Teacher A and Teacher B, both seventh grade English teachers, are required to give this same reading test in September (as a pre-test) and in June (as a post-test) to measure the achievement of their students. Look at the scores of five students in each of the two classes and see the role that standard error can play:

	Teacher A		Teacher B	
	Pre	Post	Pre	Post
Student 1	6.9	7.2	6.6	6.3
Student 2	6.8	7.1	6.8	6.5
Student 3	7.1	7.3	7.0	6.7
Student 4	7.2	7.5	7.1	6.8
Student 5	3.6	8.5	3.7	1.1

Which group of students has done better, those of Teacher A or Teacher B? Neither. Remove student number five for the moment, and look at the other four students. The standard of error of + or - .3 weighs heavily in this example. The test maker is acknowledging that .3 can be added to or subtracted from the score of each student. Consequently, results could be dramatically altered.

What about student number five in each of the classes? Extreme scores — those that are very high, very low, or show huge gains or losses — have very little reliability and should be heavily investigated using alternative forms of assessment. Extreme scores are extrapolated from a very small percentage of the sample population upon which a test is normed. For example, if the number in the sample population is four hundred students, raw scores from about 13 students (less than 3%), are used as the basis for the lowest norms. The same is true with the highest norms—they represent the scores of less than 3% of the sample population.

One final note about standard error of measurement: do not confuse it with standard deviation — they are not the same!

> Extreme scores — those that are very high, very low, or show huge gains or losses — have very little reliability and should be heavily investigated using alternative forms of assessment.

Standard deviation is a statistical measure showing degree of dispersion in a distribution of scores. "The standard deviation is a unit of measurement that shows by how much the separate scores tend to differ from the mean" (Weirsma & Jurs, 1990, p. 110). The standard deviation is most helpful when the goal is to compare scores from different tests.

Types of Tests

It is also important for educators to have an understanding of the different types of tests that are used in schools as well as the purposes of each. When determining whether or not a test is right for a certain group of students, knowledge of what the publisher intends the test to measure is vital; only then can it be determined whether or not the instrument has the necessary content validity. This information is generally located in the scoring/interpretation manual that accompanies a test. Unfortunately, test selection decisions are usually limited to a select few in each school district. Teachers are often omitted from the test selection process; as a result, they are unable to assist in determining what is best for students.

A *criterion-referenced test* measures development of a particular skill in relationship to absolute mastery. Rather than comparing an individual's performance to the performance of his or her peers, a criterion-referenced test measures whether or not the student has mastered a particular skill. Criterion-referenced tests provide answers to specific questions such as "Does Mary know that the "a" in cat has a short vowel sound?" Minimum competency tests are often criterion-referenced; if students score above a certain score, they pass. A criterion-referenced test looks at the student as an individual rather than as part of a group that is being compared to another group.

A *norm-referenced test* measures an individual's performance in relationship to that of a norm (normal) group. "The emphasis is on the relative standing of individuals rather than on absolute mastery of content" (Salvia & Ysseldyke, 1991, p. 32). In other words, an individual's score is interpreted by comparing it to the scores of a sample group. Standardized achievements tests such as the Comprehensive Test of Basic Skills and the Iowa Test of Basic Skills are examples of norm-referenced tests.

A *survey test/achievement test* is one that measures development or general achievement in one particular content area (for example, reading). The Gates-MacGinite Reading Test is an example of a survey/achievement test. The purpose of this type of test is to

> Teachers are often omitted from the test selection process; as a result, they are unable to assist in determining what is best for students.

provide a rough index of the achievement of a group of students. Survey/achievement tests are not designed with the intent to measure the growth in performance of an individual, but they are often misused in such a way.

A *direct writing assessment* is one that uses actual samples of the student's writing to judge writing ability. The scoring of a direct writing assessment requires trained readers and a carefully constructed rubric. An *indirect writing assessment*, on the other hand, measures the student's ability to recognize effective grammar, sentence construction, and paragraph organization through objective test questions. Indirect writing measures (language mechanics, language expression) constitute a large portion of most common test batteries and will be discussed in detail in the next section. It is important to note that the direct writing assessment is growing in popularity as a highly valid measure of a student's ability to effectively write in various domains. Writing domains include autobiographical incident, controversial issue, evaluation, biography, interpretation, observational, problem and solution, reflective, report of information, speculation, and story.

A *test battery* consists of a group of tests with each test in the group standardized by using the same norm-referenced population; this allows the test scores to be comparable. The most widely used test batteries include the following:

> California Achievement Test (CAT)
> Metropolitan Achievement Test (MAT)
> Comprehension Test of Basic Skills (CTBS)
> Iowa Test of Basic Skills (ITBS)
> Stanford Achievement Test (SAT)
> Texas Assessment of Academic Skills (TAAS).

Tables 1 and 2 on pages 12 and 13 give an overview of the content of each of these popular achievement batteries for grade level three. Tables 3 and 4 on pages 14 and 15 present a content analysis for the middle school test batteries. These content analysis tables will prove especially useful when integrating test preparation lessons into the curriculum.

> **It is important, to note that the direct writing assessment is growing in popularity as a highly valid measure of a student's ability to effectively write in various domains.**

Table 1: Content Analysis of CAT, CTBS, and ITBS
Grade Level 3

CAT (Fourth Edition)	CTBS (Revised)	ITBS (Fourth Edition)
Word Analysis ✔ Sounds ✔ Compounds ✔ Prefixes/Suffixes ✔ Root Words	**Word Analysis** ✔ Sounds ✔ Compounds ✔ Prefixes/Suffixes ✔ Root Words	
Vocabulary ✔ Synonyms/Antonyms ✔ Multiple Meanings ✔ Affixes ✔ Context	**Vocabulary** ✔ Synonyms/Antonyms ✔ Multiple Meanings ✔ Affix Meanings ✔ Context	**Vocabulary** ✔ Vocabulary Skills
Reading Comprehension ✔ Stories ✔ Critical Reading	**Reading Comprehension** ✔ Stories ✔ Fact and Opinion ✔ Critical Reading	**Reading Comprehension** ✔ Selections/Questions
Spelling	**Spelling**	**Spelling**
Language Mechanics ✔ Capitalization ✔ Punctuation	**Language Mechanics** ✔ Capitalization ✔ Punctuation	**Language Arts** ✔ Capitalization ✔ Punctuation ✔ Usage and Expression ✔ Sentences/Paragraphs
Language Expression ✔ Usage ✔ Sentences/Paragraphs	**Language Expression** ✔ Usage ✔ Sentences/Paragraphs	
Math Computation ✔ Addition ✔ Subtraction ✔ Multiplication ✔ Division	**Math Computation** ✔ Addition ✔ Subtraction ✔ Multiplication ✔ Division	**Math Computation** ✔ Addition ✔ Subtraction ✔ Multiplication ✔ Division
Math Concepts/Application ✔ Numeration ✔ Geometry ✔ Measurement ✔ Problem Solving	**Math Concepts/Application** ✔ Numeration ✔ Geometry ✔ Measurement ✔ Problem Solving	**Math Concepts/Applications** ✔ Concepts/Estimation ✔ Problem Solving ✔ Data Analysis
	Work-Study Skills ✔ Outlining ✔ Schedules ✔ Maps and Graphs ✔ Catalog Cards ✔ Reference Sources ✔ Guide Words	**Work-Study Skills** ✔ Alphabetizing ✔ Parts of a Book ✔ Table of Contents ✔ Maps

Table 2: Content Analysis of MAT, SAT, and TAAS
Grade Level 3

MAT (Fourth Edition)	SAT	TAAS
	Word Analysis ✔ Beginning Sounds ✔ Middle/Ending Sounds ✔ Vowel Sounds ✔ Syllabication	**Language Arts** ✔ Sentences ✔ Usage ✔ Writing Mechanics ✔ Informative Writing ✔ Narrative Writing
Vocabulary Skills ✔ Synonyms/Antonyms ✔ Multiple Meanings	**Vocabulary** ✔ Word Meanings ✔ Context Clues ✔ Multiple Meanings	
Reading Comprehension ✔ Stories/Questions	**Reading Comprehension** ✔ Stories ✔ Listening	**Reading Comprehension** ✔ Vocabulary ✔ Supporting Ideas ✔ Main Idea ✔ Relationships ✔ Inferences ✔ Reality/Fantasy
Spelling	**Spelling**	
Language Mechanics ✔ Capitalization ✔ Punctuation	**Language Mechanics** ✔ Usage ✔ Capitalization ✔ Punctuation	
Language Expression ✔ Usage ✔ Sentences/Paragraphs	**Language Expression** ✔ Sentence Structure ✔ Sentence Combining	
Math Computation ✔ Addition ✔ Subtraction ✔ Multiplication ✔ Division	**Math Computation** ✔ Addition ✔ Subtraction ✔ Multiplication ✔ Division	**Math Operation** ✔ Addition ✔ Subtraction ✔ Multiplication ✔ Division
Math Concepts/Application ✔ Estimation ✔ Problem Solving	**Math Concepts/Application** ✔ Numeration ✔ Number Theory ✔ Geometry ✔ Measurement ✔ Problem Solving	**Problem Solving** ✔ Estimation
Work-Study Skills ✔ Parts of a Book ✔ Alphabetizing ✔ Dictionary Skills ✔ Reference Sources	**Work-Study Skills** ✔ Alphabetizing ✔ Referencing Skills ✔ Dictionary Skills ✔ Parts of a Book	

Table 3: Content Analysis of CAT, CTBS, and ITBS
Middle School Level

CAT (Fourth Grade) Grade 8	CTBS (Revised) Grade 8	ITBS (Fourth Edition) Grade 8
Vocabulary ✔ Synonyms/Antonyms ✔ Words in Context ✔ Derivations	**Vocabulary** ✔ Synonyms/Antonyms ✔ Words in Context ✔ Derivations ✔ Affix Meanings ✔ Multiple Meanings	**Vocabulary** ✔ Vocabulary Skills
Reading Comprehension ✔ Passages/Questions	**Reading Comprehension** ✔ Selections ✔ Critical Reading	**Reading Comprehension** ✔ Selections/Questions
Spelling	**Spelling**	**Spelling**
Language Mechanics ✔ Capitalization ✔ Punctuation	**Language Mechanics** ✔ Capitalization ✔ Punctuation	**Language Arts** ✔ Capitalization ✔ Punctuation ✔ Usage and Expression ✔ Sentence/Paragraphs
Language Expression ✔ Usage ✔ Sentence Study ✔ Paragraphs	**Language Expression** ✔ Usage ✔ Sentence Forms ✔ Sentence Parts ✔ Sentence Combining ✔ Paragraph Study	
Math Computation ✔ Addition ✔ Subtraction ✔ Multiplication ✔ Division	**Math Computation** ✔ Addition ✔ Subtraction ✔ Multiplication ✔ Division	**Math Computation** ✔ Addition ✔ Subtraction ✔ Multiplication ✔ Division
Math Concepts/Application ✔ Numeration ✔ Geometry ✔ Measurement ✔ Problem Solving	**Math Concepts/Application** ✔ Numeration ✔ Geometry ✔ Measurement ✔ Problem Solving	**Math Concepts/Applications** ✔ Concepts/Estimation ✔ Problem Solving ✔ Data Analysis
Work-Study Skills ✔ Outlines ✔ Bibliography ✔ Library Skills	**Work-Study Skills** ✔ Outlining ✔ Index ✔ Maps and Graphs ✔ Catalog Cards	**Work-Study Skill** ✔ Key Terms

Table 4: Content Analysis of MAT, SAT, and TAAS
Middle School Level

Math (Fourth Edition) Grade 8	SAT Grade 8	TAAS Grade 7
Vocabulary Skills ✔ Synonyms/Antonyms ✔ Multiple Meanings	**Vocabulary** ✔ Word Meanings ✔ Context Clues ✔ Multiple Meanings	
Reading Comprehension ✔ Stories/Questions	**Reading Comprehension** ✔ Stories ✔ Listening	**Reading Comprehension** ✔ Vocabulary ✔ Supporting Ideas ✔ Main Idea ✔ Relationships/Outcomes ✔ Generalizations ✔ Inferences ✔ Evaluation
Spelling	**Spelling**	
Language Mechanics ✔ Capitalization ✔ Punctuation	**Language Mechanics** ✔ Usage ✔ Capitalization ✔ Punctuation	**Language Arts** ✔ Sentences ✔ Usage ✔ Writing Mechanics ✔ Writing to Inform ✔ Writing to Describe ✔ Writing for Classification ✔ Writing to Persuade ✔ Writing to Compare
Language Expression ✔ Usage ✔ Sentences/Paragraphs	**Language Expression** ✔ Sentence Structure ✔ Sentence Combining	
Math Computation ✔ Addition ✔ Subtraction ✔ Multiplication ✔ Division	**Math Computation** ✔ Addition ✔ Subtraction ✔ Multiplication ✔ Division ✔ Ratios and Percents	**Math Operation** ✔ Addition ✔ Subtraction ✔ Multiplication ✔ Division
Math Concepts/Application ✔ Estimation ✔ Problem Solving	**Math Concepts/Application** ✔ Numeration ✔ Number Theory ✔ Geometry ✔ Measurement ✔ Problem Solving	**Problem Solving** ✔ Estimation ✔ Strategies ✔ Reasonable Answers
Work-Study Skills ✔ Index ✔ Parts of a Book ✔ Dictionary Skills ✔ Reference Sources	**Work-Study Skills** ✔ Dictionary Skills ✔ Reference Skills ✔ Parts of a Book ✔ Card Catalog ✔ Reference Resources ✔ Outlines	

An additional test battery that is sometimes used at the middle school level for standardized testing in grade eight is the *New Jersey Early Warning Test* (NJEWT). Table 5 details the subtests of this language arts and math battery.

Table 5: Content Analysis *NJEWT* Grade Level 8

Reading Comprehension	Spelling	Language Mechanics
✔ Narrative Text ✔ Informational Text ✔ Persuasive Text ✔ Everyday Text	✔ Spelling Demons	✔ Capitalization and Punctuation
Language Expression ✔ Usage ✔ Sentence Completion ✔ Sentence Construction ✔ Transitions	**Writing Tasks** ✔ Solving a Problem ✔ Cause and Effect ✔ Opinion	**Math Concepts and Applications** ✔ Operations ✔ Measurement ✔ Geometry ✔ Patterns and Relationships ✔ Data Analysis ✔ Pre-Algebra

For detailed information about additional levels and the content of the subtests of each of these batteries, the series *How to Prepare Your Students for Standardized Tests* (Primary, Intermediate, and Middle School editions) by Julia Jasmine, Teacher Created Materials., Inc., is an excellent resource.

A *constructed-response item test* requires students to supply their own responses rather than select them. These usually fall into two categories, *short answer* and *essay*. A *short answer* response is one that can be scored objectively; there is a single correct answer for each item so that readers who score the test are able to agree on the correctness of each response. The following is an example of a short answer, constructed-response item:

> If oranges are priced at 18 cents each, how much would 16 oranges cost?
>
> Answer: _____

An *essay item* is one that requires the student to formulate a response, selecting ideas and presenting them according to his or her own writing style, organization, and wording. The advantages to an essay response are clear—measurement of critical thinking.

reasoning behind a response, consideration of cultural frame of reference, and reflection of higher-level learning outcomes. The disadvantage is, of course, obvious—standardization of the scoring procedure. Inconsistency in reader scoring can limit test reliability. Efforts at training readers to follow a rubric, a prescribed scoring formula that lists content and language mechanics expectations for each score value, and achieve consistency and objectivity in scoring are showing promise.

An *objective test*, or *selected-response item test,* is one that has a predetermined answer and a standard by which a response must be scored. "They are objective in the sense that attitudes, opinions, and idiosyncrasies of the examiner do not affect scoring; any two examiners would score a response in the same way" (Salvia & Ysseldyke, 1991, p. 33). Do not be misled by the term *objective*; it is not a synonym for *fair*; rather, "it implies only predetermined criteria and standardized scoring procedures" (Salvia & Ysseldyke, 1991, p. 33). The following is an example of an objective, selected-response item:

> **First, objective tests do not measure the reasoning, the "why" of an answer, no matter how clever that answer might be.**

---

1. The capital of California is

   A. Los Angeles

   B. Sacramento

   C. San Diego

It is important to understand two widespread misconceptions about objective tests. First, objective tests do not measure the reasoning, the "why" of an answer, no matter how clever that answer might be. It is a right answer or a wrong answer, period! Cultural frame of reference plays an important role here. The test maker may label an object by a term that is not part of a child's experience, resulting in a missed item even though the child's reasoning was correct. For example, is the item a sofa, a couch, a divan, or a davenport? It is what a child's family and peers, his or her part of the world, labels it! Each is correct, but all may not be within the scope of a child's frame of reference.

Also, it is a commonly held belief that objective tests are very literal, that they measure only rote skills, but this is not necessarily so. A good objective test is one that requires a wide range of skills including critical and creative thinking. "The notion that multiple choice tests can tap only recall is a myth. In fact, the best multiple choice items can—and do—measure students' ability to analyze, synthesize information, make comparisons, draw inferences, and evaluate ideas, products, or performances" (Worthen & Spandel, 1991, p. 67).

A *power test* is one that is designed to measure ability rather than rate of ability. Do not be misled, though; most power tests are timed. This seems like a contradiction in terms—a power test measures ability and not speed, but it is timed! The publisher is making the statement that based upon the norm-referenced sample, a student *should* be able to complete the test in the time allowed.

Concluding Remarks

There are many additional terms that accompany testing, but those discussed above are the most common . . . yet commonly the most misconstrued. Understanding reliability, content validity, and score extrapolations is crucial if educators hope to use standardized instruments wisely and correctly. Before continuing with the next section, check responses for the *Test Your Knowledge of Standardized Testing* items on page 3: 1 (True); 2 (True) 4 (True); 5 (False); 8 (False); 9 (True); 11 (False). Take a few moments to review related concepts if additional clarification is needed.

Understanding reliability, content validity, and score extrapolations is crucial if educators hope to use standardized instruments wisely and correctly.

Basic Principles of Standardized Testing

Aims
Several basic considerations must underlie the use of standardized testing to ensure the appropriate use of the process as an assessment procedure.

- *Access and Success*

Standardized tests should not be used to deny access; rather, they should be used as only a small part of a multifaceted assessment designed to guarantee student success. Probably the most profound negative effect of a standardized achievement measurement on students "may be the consequent limitation of educational opportunities for those who do not perform well on the tests" (Meisels, Dorfman & Steele, 1995, p. 247).

- *Equity*

A standardized test should be fair to all who take it. It should be impartial. It should be appropriate for every child regardless of gender, race, culture, or social class.

- *Curriculum Driven*

The use of a standardized test should be "congruent with the aims of the system, the school, and the curriculum" (Ruddell, 1997, p. 207). A standardized test must have content validity; it should measure what students know, not what they do not know.

> Standardized tests should not be used to deny access; rather, they should be used as only a small part of a multifaceted assessment designed to guarantee student success.

Tests that are used to measure standards or performance must be carefully analyzed for content and objectives parallel to those that have been taught.

• *Appropriate Use*
Standardized tests should only be used for the purpose for which they are intended. A test that is designed to compare a group of students to a norm-referenced sample should not be used to measure individual achievement. A test that is designed only for placement should not be used to measure progress.

• *Inclusive*
Teachers, parents, and students need to have choice as well as voice in the standardized testing practices that are employed in local as well as national assessment programs. The content and relevance of a standardized test is equally important to all who are affected by its outcomes.

• *Interactive*
Testing should be integrated with teaching. Thinking and problem-solving skills need to be developed, and testing skills need to be contextualized in meaningful instruction.

• *Broad in Scope*
Standardized tests must measure a broad curriculum, one that encourages higher-order thinking, reading, and writing. Social studies, fine arts, leisure reading, performing arts, and cooperative, project-based instruction should not fall victims to a need to teach to the test.

• *Teacher Friendly*
Accountability practices should not force teachers to adopt instructional methods they think are inappropriate to students' learning needs. Neither should they make teachers feel degraded or embarrassed because of low scores or put them in a position where they must set aside their professional judgement about what is best for a student.

> *"When teaching language arts, the teacher is not aiming to make children literate or (unless harassed) to have them score higher on a literacy test, but rather to help them gain command of the components of language and communication. The teacher sees education in terms of mastery of specific knowledge and sophistication in the performance of specific tasks, not in terms of literacy or the many psychological traits commonly defined by our tests" (Stake, 1991, p. 245).*

Accountability practices should not force teachers to adopt instructional methods they think are inappropriate to students' learning needs.

"It seems likely that the most intellectually able teachers and those with the greatest sense of professional identity will leave teaching because of the conflict; those who remain will tend to protect themselves from the dissonance by caring less about their teaching and their students" (Shepard, 1991, p. 234).

- *Student Friendly*

The primary purpose of a standardized test should be to improve and support student learning. "Tests that do not accommodate crucial differences between groups of children...are inherently inequitable. They do not give all children a fair chance to succeed, because they assume that all children come to the testing situation with roughly the same experiences, experiences that are crucial for success on standardized assessments" (Meisels, et al., 1995, p. 243)

Cautions

Standardized test scores can be helpful to the classroom teacher as well as the students who take the tests. They must, however, be used with care. They are not foolproof and do have specific limitations. Teachers must be cautious; it should never be assumed that a standardized test is reliable or valid.

There are numerous reasons why a standardized test might provide inaccurate scores in measuring development or achievement.

- *Issues of Validity*

A score may lose validity at certain age levels or competence levels. For instance, a test may fail to measure adequately the abilities of a highly competent student because its ceiling is too low. Or, conversely, some tests use a scoring system that treats the lowest group of scores as a single entity. The Nelson-Denny Reading Test, for example, states that any raw score below thirty (30) is equivalent to a grade level of 4.1. In other words, a student who scored one (1) correct on the comprehension section would get the same grade equivalent score as a person scoring 30. That is a wide range to compute to a single grade equivalent!

The predictive validity of standardized tests is also questionable. Standardized tests are not good predictors of later accomplishments. "Research indicates that neither employability nor earnings are significantly affected by students' scores on tests of basic skills..." (Hammond, 1991, p. 223).

> The primary purpose of a standardized test should be to improve and support student learning.

• *Issues of Reliability*

Comparable forms (for example, Form A and Form B) of the same test may not be parallel, thereby failing to show accurate gains or losses. Even though the test manual claims alternate form reliability, teachers often intuitively know that one form is harder for the students to do than the other form.

• *Issues of Student Performance*

Student guessing may unduly raise scores. Randomly filling in all of the blanks before time runs out will also affect the ***accuracy factor***. Take a reading comprehension test, for example, with a possible raw score of 48. Make inferences about the following scores:

	Raw Score
Mary	24
John	17
Benny	10

Any inferences that can be made are limited by the small amount of information available. It looks like John and Benny have poorer skills than Mary and that Benny has serious reading comprehension problems. Take a second look, however, and this time consider the ***accuracy factor***:

	Raw Score	Number Attempted	Accuracy Factor
Mary	24	48	50%
John	17	34	50%
Benny	10	11	91%

Benny got all but one of those he did correct. Why is he reading so slowly? Could English be his second language? If so, he does not necessarily have a reading problem; rather, he needs longer to interpret. Or, could Benny have a vision problem? Something is causing him to read slowly but accurately. Did Mary guess? She completed all of the questions, but she only got half of them right. Perhaps she randomly filled in the blanks. Does she have a reading problem? Further assessment will be necessary. John did not randomly fill in all of the blanks because he did not finish. He only got half of what he did correct, so there is some type of reading problem present.

The student's speed of work may affect the score, as indicated by the slow, thorough, and accurate student who completes only a portion of the test and thereby gets a low score. Also, students who read English as a second language may be unfairly penalized by time restraints.

The student's speed of work may affect the score as indicated by the slow, thorough, and accurate student who completes only a portion of the test and thereby gets a low score.

Finally, an individual's performance differs from day to day because of extraneous causes (lack of sleep, sickness, hunger, etc.); it is also affected by environmental factors (large, noisy group setting, students who don't take the test seriously, etc.).

- *Issues Related to the Norm-Referenced Sample*

The norms for evaluating the score may be based on a population not comparable with the students taking the test. Carefully read the norms that accompany the test. What population was used for the norm-referencing? Gender, ethnicity, age, and socio-economic characteristics of the sample population should represent the same diversity as the population that a school or district is intending to test.

- *Copyright Date*

The norms, content, and language of a standardized test become outdated very quickly. Use a current test, one that has been recently copyrighted or revised. School district demographics change rapidly; an outdated test is a sure way to raise the issue of bias.

- *Issues of Multiple Intelligences and Learning Styles*

Only a limited number of skills are measured by any one test. Most tests do not consider learning styles or multiple intelligences. Because of the way the tests are constructed, they ignore a great many kinds of knowledge and types of performance that we expect from students, and they place test-takers in a passive, reactive role, rather than engage their capacities to structure tasks, generate ideas, and solve problems (Wigdor & Garner, 1982).

Harmful Effects

There are also several reasons why standardized testing might be harmful to students as well as educational outcomes.

- *Issues of Self-Esteem*

Knowledge of low scores may be devastating to the already low self-concept of an at-risk student. Standardized tests "are not suitable for all students and can be extremely stressful for some. In addition, they can negatively affect such personality characteristics as self-concept and self-esteem" (Madaus, 1991, p. 229).

- *Issues of Expectations*

Knowledge of low scores may lower teacher expectations (No wonder he is doing so poorly, his scores are so low.) as well as student expectations (I can't do this assignment, I'm not good at math!).

Gender, ethnicity, age, and socio-economic characteristics of the sample population should represent the same diversity as the population that a school or district is intending to test.

"Poor performance on such tests is a matter of great consequences to young children. These tests have the power to alter one's own and others' perceptions of one's abilities, and to help set in motion a cycle of lower expectations" (Meisels, et al., 1995, p. 244).

- *Issues of Opportunity*

Testing "limits student's opportunities to learn because it is used as a means to track and retain students—practices that have been shown to produce lower achievement, lower self-esteem, and higher dropout rates" (Lieberman, 1991, p. 219).

- *Issues of Curriculum*

Preparation for standardized testing can lead to a teaching emphasis on literal, basic skills while ignoring higher-order critical thinking. "Rather than finding these tests an aid to good teaching and a means to be held accountable for it, teachers find that their professional judgement and their ability to provide good instructions are inhibited by the need to teach students to succeed on multiple-choice tests" (Lieberman, 1991, p. 220).

- *Issues of Equity*

Standardized testing affects issues of equity. Lower scoring students are often tracked into basic programs that lack challenges, retained in a grade, and even denied a high school diploma. "High-stakes tests can force students to leave school before they have to take the examination—or after failing it" (Madaus, 1991, page 229). According to Shepard and Smith in *Flunking Grades: Research and Policies on Retention* (as cited in Meisels, et al., 1995):

> *Testing days were particularly anxiety-provoking for those students for whom school achievement did not come easily. The performance of these children determined whether they would be admitted to fourth grade. They knew this, their teacher knew this, and their parents knew this. This was truly a high-stakes situation, with potentially long-term implications, given the accumulated knowledge about the negative impact of grade retention (p. 245).*

Lower scoring students are often tracked into basic programs that lack challenges, retained in a grade, and even denied a high school diploma.

Questions to Ask

Teachers should always evaluate a standardized test that they are asked to administer. In *Questions to Ask When Evaluating Tests*, a report funded by the U.S. Department of Education, Lawrence Rudner (1994) includes the following items in his list of questions:

> ✔ Is the test appropriate for its intended purpose?
>
> ✔ Is the test appropriate for your students and your curriculum?
>
> ✔ How close is the content of the test to the content/instruction of your students?
>
> ✔ Is the sample used for test validation and norming comparable to your students?
>
> ✔ Is the sample size large enough that you have faith in the results? Does the test have reliability?
>
> ✔ Are there detailed instructions for administration of the test?
>
> ✔ Are there resources to aid in interpretation of test results?
>
> ✔ Is the test biased or offensive with regard to race, sex, native language, ethnic origin, geographic region or other factors?
>
> ✔ Is the test appropriate for students who speak English as their second language?

Standardized tests should be used to help students succeed, not as a hindrance to learning, progress, or placement.

Concluding Remarks

Standardized tests should be used to help students succeed, not as a hindrance to learning, progress, or placement. "Evidence is now accumulating that many educational treatments involving testing for placement are not efficacious for many students (particularly minorities and the poor), have harmful side effects, and reduce opportunities to learn" (Madaus, 1991, p. 227).

By now, it should be evident that the reliability and validity of standardized tests are always questionable; the answer to number three on *Test Your Knowledge of Standardized Testing* should, therefore, be False. The answers to six and seven are also False.

Preparing to Administer a Standardized Test

Practice Makes Perfect

Is it ethical for teachers to "teach to the test"? Yes! In fact, it would be unethical if teachers did not do their best to help students be as successful as possible. At some point, however, an unmarked boundary can be crossed, and teaching to the test becomes inappropriate. As stated in *Preparing Students for Standardized Testing: One District's Perspective,* a study by Ligon and Jones (as cited in Mehrens, 1989), teaching to the test is appropriate when it "contributes to students' performing on the test near their true achievement levels, and...contributes more to their scores than would an equal amount of regular classroom instruction" (1982, page 1). "Test preparation activities by educators can range from doing nothing to providing students with copies of the tests and/or answers. The first is irresponsible; the second is unethical" (Hall & Keline, 1991, p. 2). Helping students become "test wise" can lead to performances that provide a more realistic view of what individuals know.

The idea that teachers can administer a standardized test to students one time during the school year and get meaningful results is preposterous! Not only will most students suffer from feelings of incompetence at not knowing what is expected of them, but their scores may in no way relate to their levels of knowledge. "Our tests do not tell us what students know; they tell us which students know the most about the particular questions asked" (Stake, 1991, p. 245). Or, they tell us which students have the most test taking savvy. After all, how can young students be expected to know how to "bubble in" the correct responses without practice? How can older students learn pacing and transfer skills without practice? As teachers, we are all too familiar with the consequences of skipping a line on the answer sheet or not erasing a response thoroughly. Yet, students are often faced not only with nervousness regarding content but with inexperience with actual test format, as well. Thus, it is imperative that teachers provide their students with practice that is directly aimed at familiarizing them with the format and content of the test they will take. Even if teachers do not have the actual test to review ahead of time, an analysis of the grade level manual, a practice test, and practice exercises will certainly be helpful. The goal of helping students prepare for a standardized test should be "for students to develop a set of skills and attitudes that enable them to understand the characteristics of the test, the process of taking tests, and the nature of the testing context. This will provide a better estimate of each student's level of performance on the attributes being tested" (Wheeler & Haertel, 1993, p. 6).

Test Success

In the series *How to Prepare Your Students for Standardized Tests,* Julia Jasmine suggests that there are three requirements that students need to meet for "Test Success." In order to do their best on a standardized test and achieve success, students need (1) a large vocabulary of sight words, (2) the mastery of certain specific test-taking skills, and (3) the ability to control stress. In addition to the needs Jasmine explores, students also need to be familiar with test format, feel at ease in the testing environment, and be encouraged by the teacher's positive attitude. The mastery of the content—the skills being tested—is also vital and will be discussed in the following chapter.

Vocabulary

Words are labels for concepts. The more words a student knows by sight, the better the chances of scoring well on a standardized test—in the word meaning section as well as the reading comprehension section. Each child needs to develop and continually expand a basic sight vocabulary. Wide reading experience is the best way of enlarging a child's stock of sight words, but planned instructional activities are also quite beneficial.

✔ Flashcards

✔ Labeling

✔ Listing (accompanying storytelling or oral discussion)

✔ Oral Discussion

Wide reading experience is the best way of continually enlarging a child's stock of sight words, but planned instructional activities are also quite beneficial.

- ✔ Concept Cards
- ✔ Building Experiential Background
- ✔ Structural Analysis (Roots, Prefixes, Suffixes)
- ✔ Synonyms and Antonyms
- ✔ Cloze
- ✔ Proper Names
- ✔ Multiple Meanings
- ✔ Word Banks
- ✔ Association with Pictures
- ✔ Newspaper Scavenger Hunts
- ✔ Word Art

Students have to juggle a test booklet, a separate answer sheet, a pencil and eraser, and worry about directions, timing, and pacing—all at the same time!

It is essential to build a word rich environment for students with daily opportunities for them to enrich, extend, and expand word knowledge and conceptional schemata. Vocabulary development should be an active part of the entire curriculum. Students will be motivated by the enthusiasm of the teacher, and they will be inspired to value words as the basis for language and learning.

Test-Taking Skills

"The skills students need at all grade levels in order to do well on standardized tests include the ability to follow complicated and often confusing directions, the ability to scale back what they know and focus on just what is asked, the ability to choose among confusing distractors (multiple-choice answers), and the ability to maintain concentration during boring and tedious repetition" (Jasmine, 1997, p. 6).

Children, especially young children and those who have never experienced a standardized test, need to practice to gain experience with test mechanics. Students have to juggle a test booklet, a separate answer sheet, a pencil and eraser, and worry about directions, timing, and pacing—all at the same time! These skill requirements take on new dimensions as children get older. Suddenly they have to work on a small, machine-scored answer sheet; they have to worry about neatness, putting the answer in the right place, carefully erasing errors, and hurrying to finish. They have to learn about "educated guessing," checking work if time permits, and remembering to correctly interpret test directions (e.g., go on to the next page, stop here, etc.).

It is important to help students become familiar with the type of information they will need to provide on the answer sheet (e.g., complete name, grade level, gender, date of birth, testing date, form of text, and school or student identification numbers); they should be allowed to practice writing this type of information prior to test day. The goal is to avoid problems and help students remained focused on the task at hand. Students should also have and know how to use a calculator and ruler if those items are allowed under testing conditions.

Students need practice pacing; this should be integrated into the curriculum on a regular basis, not just for test practice. Students need help in learning how to budget their time for various tasks. Students should practice "the process of elimination" when they aren't quite sure of the correct answer. Older students can be taught to look for "concrete words," (words that you can't get out of!) such as always, all, never, everyone, and none. Students should be taught that answers with terms such as these are nearly always wrong. In addition, students need to know that it is okay to guess, especially if it is an informed guess, not just a random choice. Students must understand that they should not change their first response unless they are absolutely certain that another answer is a better choice. Sometimes they will remember facts or find information in another test item that makes them firmly suspect they have made an incorrect choice. Then, and only then, an answer should be changed. Otherwise, test-wiseness dictates that their first answer is usually the best response.

> A continuum of test preparation practices is necessary to ensure a student's best performance on test day.

Students need test-taking skills that will allow them to concentrate on answering questions without becoming confused by the mechanics of the test. In a Journal of Reading article entitled *"A Study of the Differences Between Instructional Practice and Test Preparation,"* Sheila McAuliffe documents the changes that occurred in one junior high school reading class as students prepared for a state-mandated test. Her study shows the discrepancies between the authentic instruction the students were used to and the rigid demands of the reading test were a shock to all involved. "Teaching test-taking skills is not a quick remedy for poor instruction and insufficient learning, but it can help the students in learning, interpersonal relationships, work activities, and other situations they will encounter throughout life" (Wheeler & Haertel, 1993, p. 10). A continuum of test preparation practices is necessary to ensure a student's best performance on test day.

Controlling Stress

Decreasing students' stress should be a primary goal of teachers during test administration. Too often, teachers themselves are so worried about student performance, behavior, and finishing in the time allotted that they become agitated and actually increase the stress level in the classroom. In fact, there is nothing more frustrating than watching students answer questions incorrectly when their knowledge level far surpasses that which is being tested. However, maintaining a calm and positive attitude will relax students and allow them to focus on showing what they know. A smile or an encouraging look from the teacher will help to decrease anxiety and reassure students that they are capable of doing an outstanding job!

Students also need to be familiar with the purpose of the test. "Individuals perform best when they understand the purpose of what they are doing or why it is important for them to do their best on a job. If students are aware of the importance of the test, both for themselves and for their school, they are more likely to perform well on the examination. Making students aware of the purposes of the testing should improve both their attitude toward the testing and their motivation" (Wheeler and Haertel, 1993, p. 7).

Prior to test day, students can share a discussion about the importance of the test.

Prior to test day, students can share a discussion about the importance of the test. They can talk about how they think they might do, and the teacher can steer them away from negative thoughts. "Students should confront the testing with a can-do attitude. They need to feel good about themselves and believe that the assessment is providing them with a fair chance to show what they know and are able to do" (Wheeler and Haertel, 1993, p. 9).

Finally, students must know that they can ask for assistance if they make a major error. It is not unusual for a student to lose his or her place and not realize it until the testing period is nearly finished. Then, the student quickly tries to correct the damage but often ends up making it worse. As test proctor, the teacher should constantly be on the lookout for problems such as these. Testing in small groups allows the teacher more contact with each student and will be discussed in detail under the heading *Testing Day Arrives* later in this chapter.

Test Format

It is important to note that teachers must adapt the format practice opportunities they utilize when a new test is adopted by their district or mandated by the state. While the content may remain the same, the format is most often different. For example, two popular second grade tests address capitalization, end punctuation, and spelling differently:

I went to the park.
- ○ Change went to wint.
- ○ Change I to i.
- ○ Change the . to a ?.
- ○ Make no changes.

Which is correct?
- ○ I went to the park
- ○ I went to the park.
- ○ i went to the park
- ○ None of the above

While the content is the same—attempting to measure how well students have mastered language mechanics and usage skills, the format is different and must therefore be practiced accordingly. There is no need to practice both, especially with younger students, as it can confuse them and decrease the likelihood that they will recognize and feel comfortable with the actual test. The teacher must simply write similar sentences and provide students with opportunities, both in whole group and individually, to review the format of the particular test they will take.

Test format also affects how an answer sheet is marked. Some have separate sections; some have more than one answer sheet; some use a response format similar to this:

1.	(A)	(B)	(C)	(D)	(E)
2.	(F)	(G)	(H)	(I)	(J)
3.	(A)	(B)	(C)	(D)	(E)

This lettering system seems to be particularly confusing to students. The teacher should carefully review the test format and answer sheet. A practice answer sheet should be made for students to review prior to test day.

Also, the teacher should review the types of marks a student might be asked to make. These include circle the answer, put an X through the answer that is wrong, put a check mark in front of the correct answer, circle the right picture, circle the wrong picture, fill in the bubble, fill in the correct letter on a separate sheet, put an X beneath the picture that is the right choice, mark the word that is closest in meaning, mark the word that is opposite in meaning, mark the word that sounds alike, write your answer in the space provided, and so forth.

> **The teacher should carefully review the test format and answer sheet.**

In *Demystifying the Test,* Gloria Hoyos talks about the importance of helping students understand the mechanics of the test. She offers the following solutions designed to lessen test intimidation:

> Use short, sample tests for practice. It is best if the content is easy so that students can concentrate on the format.
>
> Use transparencies of the different kinds of questions students will encounter.
>
> Make a practice "question" booklet for each student; use this for daily practice question format (1996, p. 65).

Environment

Teacher attitude, testing schedule, and physical location all play a role in the testing environment.

In addition to being familiar with the format of the test being taken, students must be comfortable in the test environment. Teacher attitude, testing schedule, and physical location all play a role in the testing environment. Unfortunately, testing can be a very stressful time for teachers. Not only do they receive pressure to produce high scoring students, they are often unfamiliar with the test being given and do not receive the materials until the very last minute. Testing weeks are often filled with before and after school staff meanings focused on testing procedures.

- Which sections of the test am I supposed to administer?
- Can I read the answer choices to students?
- What if we do not finish in the time allotted?
- Do I test my special needs students?
- What about my students who have limited or no English language skills?
- How do I handle makeups for absent students?

Unfortunatley, these issues often create high levels of stress that transfer right to the students as they enter the classrooms.

The issue of the **testing schedule** also needs to be considered. Rather than changing a regular schedule to accommodate testing requirements, it is better to mold the classroom routine into a working testing schedule. Many students have trouble adapting to a simple change like the time of recess or the learning center they are to attend first in the morning, yet teachers often change the entire daily agenda in order to accommodate the needs of testing. While minor changes are inevitable, the best approach is to incorporate and practice any changes before the actual testing week. For instance, if the teacher decides to give two whole-group tests each morning, beginning with reading and then math, the schedule should be implemented several weeks in advance to provide practice for the students. That way, students will be familiar with daily expectations and can focus on a more important issue—the test! This also augments the integration of testing content and practice in curriculum goals.

The **location of testing** is another critical factor to consider. Many teachers mistakenly decide to move students about in order to combine groups according to grade level. This is a popular decision where combination or multi–age classrooms exist, as teachers decide it will be easier on everyone involved to simply test one grade level of students at a time. Two teachers of classes that contain both third and fourth grade students might, for example, feel that students will have an easier time completing their tests if one teacher administers only the third grade test to the third grade students while the other handles only the fourth grade test and students. Regardless of the benefits to the teachers involved, it is strongly recommended that this not be done, as it is difficult, if not impossible, for students to immediately respond to a new "testing" teacher. In addition, the changes in the physical environment, i.e., the new classroom setting, are likely to be a disturbance and stimulation that is not needed. Experience has proven that students test best when the test is administered by their regular classroom teacher. They are comfortable with the teacher's expectations, management system, instructional strategies, and physical environment.

> **Experience has proven that students test best when the test is administered by their regular classroom teacher.**

Many teachers also decide to administer the test in an alternative location. For instance, if a classroom is near the auditorium or gets too hot in the afternoon, it sounds reasonable to move to another place in the school for test-taking purposes. However, this is apt to bring about more negative results than positive unless proper precautions are taken. If the teacher decides to test in an alternative location, it is crucial to work with students in that location on a regular basis beforehand. Testing should not move to the multipurpose room because it appears more quiet and out of the way unless practice tests are also given in that area. Students will be distracted and enthralled with the new physical stimulus during their first few visits, and it is important that they focus all energy on the test when the time comes.

Testing Day Arrives

Consideration should be given to the best arrangement for grouping students. Middle school teachers often have the constraints of a schedule revolving around 50-or 60-minute time periods. Since many students take electives, middle school teachers must be sure that the time slated for testing is one where all students will be present. As a result, the required English class or homeroom is generally the time of choice. While it should be the responsibility of all of the content area teachers to integrate testing strategies and subject matter mastery into their instruction on a regular basis, the teacher who will administer the test should also make an effort to make students test-wise and to motivate them to do their best. Two final notes of caution to middle school teachers: don't attempt unique scheduling on test day unless it is practiced several times in advance. Also, never test students in large groups in the cafeteria or multipurpose room; results can be dismal.

Many teachers are now opting to test students in small groups, as experience and research have proven that students do best when working and learning in small groups. If the decision is made to try a small group approach, the schedule must be implemented early with test preparation lessons in small groups.

While some teachers will revert to the traditional whole-group testing procedures, do not be fooled! Most tests do not dictate a whole group or small group format. They simply give a time allotment and limit exactly what the teacher can say. It is left up to the teacher to determine how the test will be presented. The best method would probably be to give each student the test individually; unfortunately, this is not possible in most situations, so many teachers are finding success with testing in small groups. Not only does small group testing allow the teacher to watch as each child processes the information, it also affords opportunity to keep students on track, provide more individualized encouragement, and monitor potential outcomes. By using a rotation model where each group rotates through a test center, the teacher can also identify problems early and address the situation before the next group begins their test.

One design that has been highly successful is the use of four learning centers, where one center serves as the testing location. Using this approach, students are grouped in four groups and rotate through the centers. If this method is chosen, it is vital that students begin working in the centers several weeks, if not more, before the actual test. During that time, one center can be the "preparation center" where the teacher works with small groups of students on the test concepts and format. While it may seem redundant to repeat the same lesson for each group on a given day,

Many teachers are now opting to test students in small groups as experience and research have proven that students do best when working and learning in small groups.

34

the benefits are numerous. The research is clear that students are able to process more information when in small groups rather than a whole class setting; the teacher is able to actually "watch" students analyze information and assess whether or not the concepts are being grasped by each student; individual examples can be used; and students are more aware of the lesson as it is going on in the classroom for a longer period of time. The teacher can then review the concepts learned in small groups with the whole class.

A sample week's plan for a primary class is diagrammed below:

Day 1	Day 2	Day 3	Day 4	Day 5
Math—Test Preparation Lesson	Math books	Math—Test Preparation Lesson	Math Game	Math—Test Preparation Lesson
Journal Writing	Storywriting with a Friend	Publication of Day 2 Cooperative story	Write a poster advertisement for a book.	Journal Writing
Listening Center and Paired Response to Theme Story	Reading Test Preparation Lesson	Reading Game	Reading Test Preparation Lesson	Story Sequencing
Free Choice Activities	Free Choice Activities	Free Choice Activities	Free Choice Activities	Free Choice Activities

Many teachers worry about the loss of control if only testing a small group of students at a time.

- Will there be behavior problems with the students who are not working with me?
- Will I face constant interruptions?
- Will the students who are testing lose concentration?

In her book *Learning Centers,* Jodi McClay speaks to these and other issues about learning centers and small group strategies. If students are new to the center approach, the answer to these questions is a definite yes! However, if students are familiar with the expectations and procedures, they are more than capable of engaging themselves in learning activities while not being directly supervised by the teacher. That is why it is crucial to begin this type of testing approach long before testing day arrives. If this model is appropriate for your instructional goals, use it all year long. The time frame for various subject areas can vary, depending on teacher and student needs. The schedule can be implemented over a two-hour period, giving each center thirty minutes and focusing on several subject areas, including math and reading. The basis is the same: the teacher can work with one small group of students at a time while others are actively participating in the process of learning!

Many teachers worry about the loss of control if only testing a small group of students at a time.

Capitalize on Human Resources

The need for additional assistance in any classroom is paramount. Teachers need help! Whether it be working with a group of students, preparing a learning center, or sharing information, help is greatly appreciated. However, the demands on today's parents have limited their time and ability to assist; likewise, limited funds have decreased the availability of paid assistants. Therefore, many teachers are going to extreme measures to obtain and train parent volunteers, paid instructional assistants, and tutors. Strategies include sending frequent requests for help to parents, calling and accepting the time a parent is available to help, training volunteers during lunch recess, teaming with teachers to share assistant time, financing paid help through alternative funds, and working with teachers at other grade levels to establish beneficial tutor schedules, guidelines, and training. Regardless of the resources available, make the best of what is provided. Keep in mind that extra adult help is not mandatory; many classrooms are highly successful with only the teacher in the room (McClay, 1996b). However, a particularly good time to arrange for parent assistance is during test preparation and testing week, especially if your district or state allows parents to supervise students out of the classroom. If this is the case, schedule parent activities that take small groups of students away from the testing environment. Just be sure to emphasize that students cannot return to the room while others are testing and that you will come for them when it is time to switch groups.

It is important to prepare students for testing by aligning test content and curriculum, teaching test-wiseness, and giving ample opportunity for students to prepare.

Concluding Remarks

It is important to prepare students for testing by aligning test content and curriculum, teaching test-wiseness, and giving ample opportunity for students to prepare. Students who are familiar with test expectations and comfortable with the testing environment will be more successful than those who are merely handed the test on testing day. It is equally important to build student self-esteem, the feeling of "I know I can," and utilize available resources as well as the best possible strategies to ensure a successful test day for every student.

Test-taking skills go beyond performance on tests and measurements. Skills such as pacing, estimating, following directions, intelligent guessing, problem solving, and risk-taking can help the students in school learning, interpersonal relationships, work activities, and many other situations they will encounter throughout life (Wheeler & Haertel, 1993, page 10).

The answer to question number 12 on *Test Your Knowledge of Standardized Testing* can be found in this chapter. Actually, it can be answered either True or False, depending on the reasoning behind the answer. It is ethical to "teach to the test" as long as test security is honored. In fact, it is vital to student success to teach to the test in a way that shows students what will be expected of them. It is not ethical to violate test security by using actual test items for practice. Neither is it ethical to abandon professional judgement about curriculum issues and teach only what will be on the test.

One final note: teachers should be sure to review *First Grade Takes a Test* by Miriam Cohen and Lillian Hoban (Bantam Doubleday Dell Publishing Group, Inc.). This is a poignant story about test anxiety and what really matters in life!

In fact, it is vital to student success to teach to the test in a way that shows students what will be expected of them.

Content of Standardized Tests: Practice and Curriculum Integration

Overview

Generally speaking, the standardized tests used in kindergarten through eighth grade are test batteries designed to measure achievement in basic skills. Those most commonly used across the grade levels are CAT, CTBS, ITBS, MAT, SAT, and TASS. The NJEWT is used for testing the high school skill readiness of eighth grade students. A growing number of school districts also use a reading survey test; the most common include Gates-MacGinite, Degrees of Reading Power, Stanford Diagnostic Reading Test, and Nelson-Denny Reading Test. For specific information and a critique about any test in print, consult the references from the Buros Institute of Mental Measurements. These include the following:

◆ *Tests in Print*

This reference contains a listing and brief description of every test that is registered with the institute. It is a cumulative reference, so it contains information about current as well as previous editions of a test.

◆ *Mental Measurement Yearbook*

There are several volumes available, but they are not cumulative. Rather, each volume contains an evaluative review of tests that are new or newly revised.

For specific information and a critique about any test in print, consult the references from the Buros Institute of Mental Measurements.

These references are available in the reference departments of most libraries. Additional information may be obtained from the Buros Institute of Mental Measurements, 135 Bancroft Hall, University of Nebraska, Lincoln, Nebraska 68588-0348. The Website location for the Buros Institute is as follows:

www.unl.edu/buros

For a moderate fee, current evaluations and reviews of any test can be ordered via Internet and immediately faxed to the requested location. This is a particularly valuable service, as teachers are often asked to make a rush decision about test selection.

Test Content

The content of standardized test batteries represents a wide range of skills including word analysis, vocabulary, spelling, language mechanics and expression, mathematical operations and concepts, and work-study skills. For an overview of the skills in each of these test batteries, review the following tables on pages 12–16:

Table Number	Standardized Batteries	Grade Level	Page Number
1	CAT CTBS ITBS	3	12
2	MAT SAT TAAS	3	13
3	CAT CTBS ITBS	8	14
4	MAT SAT TAAS	8 7	15
5	NJEWT	8	16

It is vital that teachers provide ample opportunities for practice of the skills required for success in each content area; it is equally important that this practice be integrated within the curriculum and daily instructional strategies rather than isolated.

The content of standardized test batteries represents a wide range of skills including word analysis, vocabulary, spelling, language mechanics and expression, mathematical operations and concepts, and work-study skills.

Word Analysis, Word Study

This type of subtest often measures basic skill development in letter recognition, letter-sound correspondence, identifying initial sounds, identifying final sounds, rhyming sounds, and word building. Higher levels of the test measure ability to identify initial, medial, and final sounds, silent letters, initial and final consonant substitution, vowel sounds, affixes, inflectional endings, and compound words.

Sample Question: Intermediate Level
Word Analysis: Vowel Sounds
Directions: Read the word with the underlined letter. Decide what vowel sound the letter makes. Then choose the word that has the same vowel sound.

> **skip**
> (A)   smile
> (B)   bird
> (C)   fill

Spelling

This type of subtest generally asks students to identify incorrectly spelled words used in sentences or to choose the correct spelling from a number of choices.

Sample Question: Primary Level
Spelling
Directions: Look at the words in Number 1. They are mother, visit, and month. Listen carefully: My mother will visit my grandparents next month. Circle the word that is not spelled correctly.

> 1.   mother   visit   munth

Vocabulary

This type of subtest can measure the student's understanding of word meanings in various ways:

- categorize words
- find a synonym, a word with a similar meaning
- find an antonym, a word with an opposite meaning
- use context to determine word meanings, especially with words that have multiple meanings

Sample Question: Intermediate Level
Vocabulary: Synonyms

Directions: Read the phrase. Look for the word that has the same or almost the same meaning as the underlined word.

<u>slight</u> change
    (A)   huge
    (B)   important
    (C)   small
    (D)   slow

Reading Comprehension

This type of subtest can assess literal, inferential, and applied comprehension (Herber, 1976) by requiring students to read sentences, short selections, and stories to derive meaning.

Literal Comprehension: **Reading the lines!** This is a "right there" answer in the text, and does not require interpretation. Details are usually literal—how many, what color, who, where, or when?

Inferential Comprehension: **Reading between the lines!** This is a "read and think" answer; facts and evidence are presented in the reading, but an interpretation must be made. An answer is implied in the reading selection, and the reader must draw a conclusion. What does the author mean? What is the author's purpose? What is the mood of the main character?

Applied Comprehension: **Reading beyond the lines!** The "reader understands unstated relationships between information in text and information in his or her prior knowledge base" (Ruddell, 1997, p. 68).

"Most standardized tests now use excerpts from content-area texts rather than narrative fiction" (Hoyos, 1996, p. 61). Page 42 shows a sample middle school level reading comprehension passage and related questions.

Reading Comprehension: Passages

Samples

Anthropology is the study of human beings. (Anthropo means humans and logy means study of.) It is concerned with all aspects of human development. Because of this broad approach, it is generally divided into two branches: cultural anthropology and physical anthropology.

Cultural anthropology is the study of people who are alive today, and it has traditionally focused on the societies of the world which have little (or at least less) technology. It is the study of the broad area of learned behavior occurring only among humans. A cultural anthropologist making a study of an Eskimo village, for example, would study clothing, food, religious practices, and a wide range of Eskimo behaviors.

Physical anthropology is the study of the biological features of humans. Physical anthropologists trace and follow the development of the bones and skulls that they find to put together the fascinating story of human variation and human development. Their study can include people who are alive today, but often it deals with people who lived and died long ago.

Because human beings are so complex, however, it is impossible to separate completely the subject matters of these two branches. The *biocultural* approach to anthropology, which combines the physical and the cultural features, offers the best overall look at human beings.

1. What is the topic of the selection?
   (A) cultural anthropology
   (B) physical anthropology
   (C) anthropology in general
   (D) anthropologists

2. Physical anthropology is concerned with . . .
   (F) all aspects of human development.
   (G) the history of human biology.
   (H) food and religious practices.
   (J) the broad area of learned behavior.

3. The author takes the position that it is impossible to completely separate physical and cultural anthropology because . . .
   (A) both branches deal with people who are alive today.
   (B) both branches deal with people who left only bones to study.
   (C) human beings are so complex.
   (D) human beings always have a culture.

4. The author's purpose in this passage is to . . .
   (F) establish a basis for considering both the physical and cultural branches of anthropology.
   (G) restrict the topic to just the physical aspects of anthropology.
   (H) restrict the topic to just the cultural aspects of anthropology.
   (J) propose an entirely new way of looking at the science of anthropology.

5. In this passage, the term *biocultural* means. . .
   (A) an approach that stresses the physical aspects of anthropology.
   (B) an approach that stresses the cultural aspects of anthropology.
   (C) a combination of the traditional and modern approaches to anthropology.
   (D) a combination of the physical and cultural approaches to anthropology.

Answers:

1	Ⓐ Ⓑ Ⓒ Ⓓ	4	Ⓕ Ⓖ Ⓗ Ⓙ
2	Ⓕ Ⓖ Ⓗ Ⓙ	5	Ⓐ Ⓑ Ⓒ Ⓓ
3	Ⓐ Ⓑ Ⓒ Ⓓ		

Reprinted from TCM 2132, How to Prepare Your Middle School Students for Standardized Tests, *Teacher Created Materials, Inc., 1997*

Language Mechanics

This subtest measures punctuation skills as well as the ability to correctly use capitalization. It is an indirect measure of a student's ability to write. Often, students are asked to edit sentences or paragraphs by identifying those places that need specific punctuation marks or capitalized letters.

Sample Question: Primary Level
Language Mechanics: Capitalization and Punctuation

Directions: Fill in the answer circle in front of the sentence that has correct capitalization and punctuation.

    ○ My shirt has a rip in it
    ○ did you remember your homework?
    ○ Marie's letter was interesting
    ○ He plays video games every day.

Language Expression

This type of subtest assesses the student's ability in using effective written English, including the use of parts of speech, the formation of sentences, and the organization of paragraphs.

Sample Question: Intermediate Level
Language Expression: Sentences

Directions: Choose the sentence that has the complete subject underlined.

    (A) Lincoln's <u>birthday</u> is in February.
    (B) <u>This glue</u> has dried up.
    (C) <u>The black</u> paper is all gone.
    (D) The winning team <u>was very</u> excited.

Mathematical Operations

This type of subtest requires students to solve addition, subtraction, multiplication, and division problems. Depending on the level of the test, students are asked to work with whole numbers, fractions, mixed numbers, decimals, and algebraic expressions.

Page 44 shows sample primary level computation problems involving division (with pictures).

Student Practice Page

Math: Computation—Division (with Pictures)

Directions: Do the sample below with your teacher. Then complete each division problem. Fill in the circle for the answer that you think is correct.

Sample

There are 6 ice cream bars in a package. A group of 3 friends wanted to share the package so that they each would get the same number of ice cream bars. How many ice cream bars would each friend get? Fill in the circle next to your answer.

○ 2
○ 3
○ 5
○ 9

1. Mario was staying in a cabin in the forest. He had 12 bottles of water. He knew he would use 2 bottles of water a day. How many days could Mario plan to stay? Fill in the circle next to your answer.

○ 2   ○ 6
○ 12   ○ 14

2. Millie mixed milk and pudding mix to make 16 ounces of pudding. Her serving dishes will each hold 4 ounces. If she fills each dish right to the top, how many dishes can she fill? Fill in the circle next to your answer.

3. Jason is putting science folders together. Each folder needs 3 brads. He has 15 3-inch brads. How many folders can he put together? Fill in the circle next to your answer.

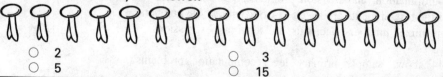

○ 2   ○ 3
○ 5   ○ 15

Reprinted from TCM 2130, How to Prepare Your Students for Standardized Tests—Primary, *Teacher Created Materials, Inc., 1997*

Mathematical Concepts

This type of subtest measures a student's ability to understand and apply a range of mathematical concepts involving numeration, number sentences, number theory, problem solving, measurement, and geometry. Problem solving requires students to work with word problems.

Sample Problem: **Intermediate Level**
Math Concepts/Applications: **Numeration**

What is the value of the 5 in 654,732?

      (A) 500
      (B) 5,000
      (C) 50,000
      (D) 500,000

Sample Problem: **Middle School Level**
Math Concepts/Applications: **Probability and Statistics**

A. This graph shows the amount of rain that fell in an area over a six-year period. What was the average yearly rainfall during this period?

YEARLY RAINFALL IN INCHES

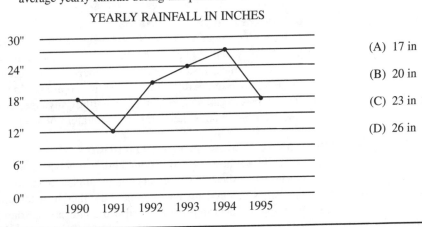

      (A) 17 in

      (B) 20 in

      (C) 23 in

      (D) 26 in

Reprinted from TCM 2132, How to Prepare Your Middle School Students for Standardized Tests, *Teacher Created Materials Inc., 1997*

Work-Study Skills

This subtest measures students' skills in using parts of a textbook, reading maps and graphs, finding words in a dictionary, and using good study techniques.

Sample Question: Intermediate Level
Word-Study Skills: Maps

This map shows the streets and buildings in a section of downtown Oakmont.

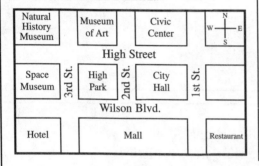

A. Which place is the farthest away from the Natural History Museum?

   (1) the hotel   (3) the city hall

   (2) the mall   (4) the restaurant

B. A visitor is standing on the southeast corner of Wilson Blvd. and 3rd Street. If she walks north across the street, where will she be?

   (1) in the park   (3) at the mall

   (2) at the hotel   (4) at the city hall

Reprinted from TCM 2132, How to Prepare Your Students for Standardized Tests—Intermediate, *Teacher Created Materials Inc., 1997*

Social Studies and Science Skills

Some test batteries contain subtests in the areas of social studies and science. In social studies, items measure understanding of geography, economics, history, political science, and sociology. Students are often asked to differentiate fact from opinion. In science, items measure understanding of scientific language, concepts, and inquiry methods; items represent all areas of science.

Integrating Practice and Curriculum

High-stakes tests, those tied to accountability practices and student placement issues, "tend to encourage undue attention to material that is covered in the examinations, thereby excluding from teaching and learning many worthwhile educational objectives and experiences" (Madaus, 1991, p. 229). Teachers need to make every effort to integrate test content mastery as well as test wiseness skills into worthwhile activities that expand, rather than decrease, educational opportunities for students. They need to utilize a wide range of subject-related materials in the everyday curriculum to ensure that students have ample opportunity to read a variety of materials and build background in a variety of subject areas. Building a rich and varied educational experience for children should include active teaching and learning strategies such as these:

- Teachers should use a variety of reading materials to expand the frame of reference and to highlight various writing styles for students. These should include

  ✔ Newspaper articles of various kinds

  ✔ Functional materials such as job applications, labels, directions for making something or installing something, directions from common cold remedies such as aspirin or cough medicine, and the local bus or train schedule

  ✔ Literature from various genres, including poetry, stories, and essays

  ✔ Books, books, and more books for a structured, daily leisure reading time

  ✔ Magazines

  ✔ Interesting pieces of text from all subject areas

- Teachers should model reading and writing strategies for their students. While students read along and listen, the teacher can work through a piece of text to interpret meaning, draw conclusions, and make judgments. The teacher should also point out transitions—words like also, in addition, on the other hand, because, instead, for example—and show how they connect sentences or paragraphs and develop relationships. Have students practice these skills in cooperative groups or teach a passage to their classmates. Older students should learn to recognize patterns of paragraph organization—listing, cause and effect, comparison and contrast, definition and example, time order or sequence—to enhance their ability to analyze, synthesize, and make applications.

- Teachers should make a habit of using test question language. What is the mood of this story? What do you think will happen next? Describe the traits of the main character. What would be a good title for this selection? What is the author's purpose? Can you support your opinion with a piece of text? What do you think will happen next? Is this a fact or an opinion? Why? Why not? Why? Why not? Why? Why? Why?

Teachers should use a variety of reading materials to expand students' frame of reference and to highlight various styles of writing.

Teach students to always apply the "**5W + 1 H**" formula to everything they read:

- ♦ **Who**
- ♦ **What**
- ♦ **When**
- ♦ **Where**
- ♦ **Why**
- ♦ **How**

- Teachers should use as many hands-on, active math teaching activities as possible. Students need to develop critical thinking and problem solving skills by interacting with the concepts, not just reading about them. They need to write their own problems, investigate, draw conclusions, collaborate, and solve.

- Teachers need to have students write, write, and write some more! Writing is a way of knowing, a way of thinking, a way of exploring. Students need to practice writing to prompts of various domains. They can write a letter that is persuasive, explore a controversial topic, evaluate a piece of literature or a television program, or tell a story. Teach prewriting strategies such as brainstorming or clustering. Encourage journal writing as a daily activity.

Writing is a way of knowing, a way of thinking, a way of exploring.

Portfolios, cooperative groups, collaborative projects, guest speakers, computer assisted instruction, Internet activities, and learning centers also provide excellent ways to integrate test content practice into classroom instructional strategies.

Authentic assessment can also facilitate in the integration of test preparation and curriculum. Authentic assessment strategies are especially useful in providing the student and teacher with benchmarks representing progress toward attainment of curriculum goals. "When assessment in ongoing, as is the case with authentic assessment, teacher and students are in a position to evaluate the learning process throughout the course of the study" (Ryan, 1994, p. 6). By utilizing authentic assessment strategies, the teacher is able to gather important information about students' mastery of the content that will later be measured via a standardized test. In addition, these strategies enable the teacher to gather portfolio information that can be shared with parents during conferences. For example, look at the grades one and two authentic assessment reading evaluation on page 50. Activities like this can help the teacher evaluate the child's literacy development, knowing that the child will be asked to complete similar tasks on a mandated standardized test. This form becomes an important addition to the child's portfolio and gives the teacher a reference point for the "Why?" that parents often ask.

Finally, in integrating content and curriculum, it is important to teach to a full range of cognitive skills. One of the major criticisms of standardized testing has been that they measure only superficial or literal knowledge. The test publishers have listened intently to this criticism and have responded with tests that better reflect the applications of skills in a variety of cognitive levels. Reprinted on pages 51–53 is an assortment of intermediate level literature activities that reach across the cognitive skill levels of Bloom's Taxonomy of Educational Objectives. An authentic assessment measure designed for literal comprehension is shown on page 54. Other types of authentic measures that facilitate the integration of test preparation with content mastery include the following:

♦ **Performance Tasks**
♦ **Rubrics**
♦ **Observation-Based**
♦ **Miscue Analysis**
♦ **Science Investigations**
♦ **Open-Ended Tasks**

Finally, in integrating content and curriculum, it is important to teach to a full range of cognitive skills.

Assessment of Reading Comprehension: Narrative Form

Student's Name _____

Age_____ Grade_____ Date _____

For this comprehension assessment, use a book with which the child is unfamiliar.

Name of book _____

Scoring Scale: 1=unsuccessful   2=moderately successful   3=successful

1. The child can retell the story, including all main events.

   Score _____

   Examples/Comments _____

2. The child can retell the story in chronological order.

   Score _____

   Examples/Comments _____

   _____

3. The child can answer questions about details in the story.

   Score _____

   Examples/Comments _____

   _____

4. The child can define words from the story.

   Score _____

   Examples/Comments _____

   _____

Reprinted from TCM 773, Language Arts Assessment, *Teacher Created Materials, Inc., 1994*

Bloom's Taxonomy Activities

On the following three pages are 40 specific literature activities listed in rising levels of difficulty, skill development, and critical thinking. These may be adapted to different types of literature, as well as providing the teacher with flexible types of activities to match the differing abilities, needs, and aspirations of students in the modern classroom. Such an overall scope and framework allows the teacher to plan with assurance that all students are provided with activities designed to develop the full range of their cognitive abilities.

Knowledge

This level provides the students an opportunity to recall fundamental facts and information about the story. Success at this level will be evidenced by the student's ability to

- match character names with pictures of the characters.

- identify the main characters in a crossword puzzle.

- match statements with the characteristics of one of the main characters in a wanted poster.

- arrange scrambled story pictures in sequential order.

- arrange scrambled story sentences in sequential order.

- recall details about the setting by creating a picture of where a part of the story took place.

Comprehension

This level provides the student an opportunity to demonstrate a basic understanding of the story. Success at this level will be evidenced by the student's ability to

- interpret pictures of scenes from the story.

- explain selected ideas or parts from the story in his or her own words.

- draw a picture showing what happened before and after a passage or illustration found in the book.

- predict what could happen next in the story before the reading of the entire book is completed.

- construct a pictorial time line which summarizes what happens in the story.

- explain how the main character felt at the beginning, middle, and/or end of the story.

Reprinted from TCM 2004, Activities for any Literature Unit Intermediate, *Teacher Created Materials, Inc., 1996*

Bloom's Taxonomy
Activities *(cont.)*

Application

This level provides the students an opportunity to use information from the story in a new way. Success at this level will be evidenced by the student's ability to

- classify the characters as human, animal, or thing.

- transfer a main character to a new setting.

- make finger puppets to act out a part of the story.

- select a meal that one of the main characters would enjoy eating; plan a menu and a method of serving it.

- think of a situation that occurred to a character in the story and write about how he or she would have handled the situation differently.

- give examples of people the student knows who have the same problems as the characters in the story.

Analysis

This level provides the student an opportunity to take parts of the story and examine these parts carefully in order to better understand the whole story. Success at this level will be evidenced by the student's ability to

- identify general characteristics (stated and/or implied) of the main characters.

- distinguish what could happen from what couldn't happen in the story in real life.

- select parts of the story that were the funniest, saddest, happiest, and most unbelievable.

- differentiate fact from opinion.

- compare and/or contrast two of the main characters.

- select an action of a main character that was exactly the same as something the student would have done.

Reprinted from TCM 2004, Activities for any Literature Unit—Intermediate, *Teacher Created Materials, Inc., 1996*

Bloom's Taxonomy
Activities *(cont.)*

Synthesis

This level provides the student with the opportunity to put parts from the story together in a new way to form a new idea or product. Success at this level will be evidenced by that student's ability to

- write three new titles for the story that would give a good idea of what it is about.
- create a poster to advertise the story so people will want to read it.
- create a new product related to the story.
- restrict the roles of the main characters to create new outcomes in the story.
- compose and perform a dialogue or monologue that will communicate the thoughts of the main characters at a given point in the story.
- imagine that he or she is one of the main characters and write a diary account of daily thoughts and activities.
- create an original character and tell how the character would fit into the story.
- write the lyrics and music to a song that one of the main characters would sing if he/she became a rock star—and then perform it.

Evaluation

This level provides the student with an opportunity to form and present an opinion backed by sound reasoning. Success at this level will be evidenced by the student's ability to

- decide which character in the selection he or she would most like to spend a day with and why.
- judge whether or not a character should have acted in a particular way and why.
- decide if the story really could have happened and justify the decision.
- consider how this story can help the student in his or her own life.
- appraise the value of the story.
- compare the story with another one the student has read.
- write a recommendation as to why the book (story) should be read or not.

Reprinted from TCM 2004, Activities for any Literature Unit—Intermediate, *Teacher Created Materials, Inc., 1996*

Use this checklist to document your observation of literal comprehension in first or second grade readers.

Individual Checklist for
Literal Comprehension in Reading
Grade 1 or 2

Name _____ Date _____

Title of Story _____

Behavior	Observed			
	Poor to Excellent			
	1	2	3	4
Can answer questions about details from the story (literal details)				
Can retell story, including all main events (main idea)				
Can retell story in chronological order (sequence)				
Can answer questions about first, last, etc. (sequence)				
Defines words from the story (vocabulary)				
Recognizes and explains effects of an affix on a word in the story (vocabulary)				

Reprinted from TCM 504, Portfolios and Other Assessments, *Teacher Created Materials Inc., 1993*

Concluding Remarks

By allowing students to actively participate in learning experiences that require various cognitive skills and assessing learning continuously through authentic measures, the teacher will have integrated instruction with assessment. In addition, opportunities will have been provided for each child to master the content and skills required for standardized testing.

> *"Teaching students test-taking skills and helping them become test-wise test-takers is not a quick remedy for poor instruction and insufficient learning, or for a weak educational program. The best way to prepare students for testing is to provide them with a solid educational program that challenges them, but in which they are able to succeed" (Wheeler & Haertel, 1993, p. 10).*

The pages that follow provide samples of practice exercises found in *How to Prepare Your Students for Standardized Tests* (Jasmine, 1997). Primary, intermediate, and middle school practices are showcased to provide a wide range of sampling, so be sure to check citations for the correct level of each sample. Primary includes grades one, two, and three; intermediate begins with grade three and continues through grade five; the middle school practices have a grade level range of five through nine.

By allowing students to actively participate in learning experiences that require various cognitive skills and assessing learning continuously through authentic measures, the teacher will have integrated instruction with assessment.

Reading Comprehension: Stories

Story 1, Page 2

Mary and Sally spent the first day of their vacation cleaning up the yard and setting up their small pool. They got out all of the pool toys. The sandbox needed new sand, but they got out the sand toys anyway. Then they wiped off the table and chairs. After a long search, they found their picnic things in the garage. The girls were <u>preparing</u> to have a wonderful summer.

5. What is the main idea of this part of the story?
   - ○ The girls were preparing to have a wonderful summer.
   - ○ The girls were bored and had nothing to do.
   - ○ The yard was a terrible mess.
   - ○ All of the toys were in the garage.

6. Where did the girls find their picnic things?
   - ○ in the pool
   - ○ in the sandbox
   - ○ in the garage
   - ○ in the yard

7. What did the girls do after they got out the sand toys?
   - ○ They cleaned up the yard.
   - ○ They wiped off the table and chairs.
   - ○ They set up the pool.
   - ○ They got out the pool toys.

8. In this story, <u>preparing</u> means . . .
   - ○ working.
   - ○ playing.
   - ○ going away.
   - ○ getting ready.

Reprinted from TCM 2130, How to Prepare Your Students for Standardized Tests—Primary, *Teacher Created Materials, Inc., 1997*

Student Practice Page ── | TS 191 |

Language Expression: Usage (Sentences)

Samples

A. Our friends_____a new car.
- ○ has
- ○ have

B. That airplane is flying too_____.
- ○ low
- ○ lower
- ○ lowly
- ○ lowest

1. We _____ a picture for each student.
- ○ is hanging
- ○ are hanging

2. Joe _____ television every evening.
- ○ watch
- ○ watches

3. The farmer has six _____ .
- ○ sheep
- ○ sheeps

4. I _____ a song after you do.
- ○ sang
- ○ will sing
- ○ sings
- ○ has sung

5. Where are _____ new gloves?
- ○ Jenny
- ○ Jennys'
- ○ Jenny's
- ○ Jennys

6. Study the answers _____ .
- ○ careful
- ○ carefully
- ○ most careful
- ○ more careful

7. _____are going to the party.
- ○ Me and Jim
- ○ Jim and me
- ○ I and Jim
- ○ Jim and I

8. That _____ tire has a nail in it.
- ○ cars
- ○ car's
- ○ cars'
- ○ cars's

9. Those girls already lost _____ tickets.
- ○ there
- ○ they're
- ○ their
- ○ them

10. I started a very _____ book.
- ○ long
- ○ longer
- ○ longest
- ○ longly

11. Fran and José _____ research.
- ○ are doing
- ○ is doing

12. Some of the _____ are broken.
- ○ drinking fountains
- ○ drinking fountain

13. I _____ them last night.
- ○ see
- ○ seen
- ○ saw
- ○ will see

14. The bus _____ right now.
- ○ is coming
- ○ are coming

15. Give the package to _____ .
- ○ .Jack and me
- ○ Jack and I

16. Your story is _____ than mine.
- ○ longer
- ○ longest
- ○ long
- ○ longly

Reprinted from TCM 2130, How to Prepare Your Students for Standardized Tests—Primary, *Teacher Created Materials Inc., 1997*

Math: Concepts/Applications—Graphs

Sample

	Dry Days
April	☀☀☀
May	☀☀☀☀☀
June	☀☀☀☀
July	☀☀☀☀
Aug.	☀☀☀
Sept.	☀☀
Each ☀ = 1 Dry Day	

A. In which month were there the fewest dry days?
- ○ April
- ○ May
- ○ August
- ○ September

B. How many more dry days were there in May than in August?
- ○ 1
- ○ 2
- ○ 3
- ○ 4

C. How many dry days were there in May and June altogether?
- ○ 4
- ○ 5
- ○ 8
- ○ 9

	Books Read
Randy	📖📖📖
Jon	📖📖📖📖
Lili	📖📖
Kris	📖
Sung	📖📖📖📖📖
Pat	📖📖📖
Each 📖 = 2 Books	

1. How many books did Lili read?
- ○ 3
- ○ 4
- ○ 5
- ○ 6

2. Which two students read the same number of books?
- ○ Randy and Pat
- ○ Jon and Sung
- ○ Lili and Kris
- ○ Randy and Lili

3. How many more books did Sung read than Kris?
- ○ 2
- ○ 4
- ○ 6
- ○ 8

4. How many books did the students read in all?
- ○ 24
- ○ 28
- ○ 40
- ○ 48

Reprinted from TCM 2130, How to Prepare Your Students for Standardized Tests—Intermediate, *Teacher Created Materials Inc., 1997*

Math Concepts/Applications: **Strategies**

Directions: Read each problem. Look for the correct answer. Fill in the answer circle for your choice.

Samples

A. Gabby bought a game. She needs to know the price of the game, but she cannot find her receipt. She remembers paying for the game with a twenty dollar bill. What other information does she need in order to figure out how much the game cost?
(A) how many pieces are in the game
(B) how much change she received
(C) how much allowance she gets
(D) how much money she gave the clerk

1. A man is driving his car at an average speed of 65 miles per hour. He drives for 4 hours. Knowing this, which one of these could you find?
(A) the number of stops he made
(B) the distance he traveled
(C) the direction in which he traveled
(D) the number of other people in the car

2. There are 38 weeks in a school year. Students attend school 6 hours a day, 5 days a week. Using this information, which one of these could you figure out?
(F) what students do on weekends
(G) hours students spend at recess each day
(H) what students do after school
(J) hours students spend in school each year

3. A certain tree adds 1/2 inch to the circumference of its trunk every year. It is 3 feet around now. How could you find out what the circumference of its trunk would in 10 years?
(A) 3 feet + (1/2 inch + 10 years)
(B) 1/2 inch + (3 feet x 10 years)
(C) 1/2 inch x 3 feet x 10 years
(D) 3 feet + (1/2 inch x 10 years)

B. Side AB is 12 units. What else do you need to know to find the area of this rectangle?
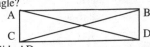
(F) Side AD
(G) Side CD
(H) Side BD
(J) Side BC

4. There were 5008 books in the school library. New books were added, making a total of 5695 books. How could you figure out how many new books were added.
(F) 5008 + 5695 = _____
(G) 5008 + _____ = 5695
(H) 5008 – _____ = 5695
(J) _____ + 5695 = 5008

5. Three fifth grade classes are going on a field trip in two buses. There are two classes of 30 students and one class of 20 students. If the teachers want an even number on each bus, what should they do?
(A) (30 + 30 + 20) ÷ 2
(B) (30 + 20) ÷ 2
(C) (30 + 20) x 2
(D) (30 + 30 + 20) x 2

6. Anderson Elementary School has 354 students. The 214 students of Winton Elementary School will join them while their school is being repaired. How many students will there be altogether?
(F) 354 ÷ 214
(G) 354 x 214
(H) 354 – 214
(J) 354 + 214

Answers: A Ⓐ Ⓑ Ⓒ Ⓓ   1 Ⓐ Ⓑ Ⓒ Ⓓ   3 Ⓐ Ⓑ Ⓒ Ⓓ   5 Ⓐ Ⓑ Ⓒ Ⓓ
      B Ⓕ Ⓖ Ⓗ Ⓙ   2 Ⓕ Ⓖ Ⓗ Ⓙ   4 Ⓕ Ⓖ Ⓗ Ⓙ   6 Ⓕ Ⓖ Ⓗ Ⓙ

Reprinted from TCM 2131, *How to Prepare Your Students for Standardized Tests—Intermediate,*
Teacher Created Materials Inc., 1997

Spelling Skills (SAT)

Directions: Look at the four words in each item. Fill in the answer circle at the bottom of the page for the word that is not spelled correctly.

Samples

A.
(A) headache
(B) diference
(C) flashlight
(D) journey

B.
(F) paint
(G) mistake
(H) mansion
(J) nowledge

1.
(A) paragraff
(B) roasted
(C) sadness
(D) reverse

6.
(F) pillow
(G) warmth
(H) storey
(J) worst

2.
(F) sometimes
(G) property
(H) kwestion
(J) section

7.
(A) bravery
(B) collored
(C) rained
(D) music

3.
(A) leppard
(B) napkin
(C) recreation
(D) climate

8.
(F) solemm
(G) fourth
(H) divide
(J) global

4.
(F) confuse
(G) bilding
(H) century
(J) beneath

9.
(A) ignore
(B) dropped
(C) obay
(D) mountain

5.
(A) around
(B) customer
(C) decorate
(D) teecher

10.
(F) mischiff
(G) pigeon
(H) peculiar
(J) magnet

Answers:

A (A) (B) (C) (D)	2 (F) (G) (H) (J)	5 (A) (B) (C) (D)	8 (F) (G) (H) (J)
B (F) (G) (H) (J)	3 (A) (B) (C) (D)	6 (F) (G) (H) (J)	9 (A) (B) (C) (D)
1 (A) (B) (C) (D)	4 (F) (G) (H) (J)	7 (A) (B) (C) (D)	10 (F) (G) (H) (J)

Reprinted from TCM 2131, How to Prepare Your Students for Standardized Tests—Intermediate, *Teacher Created Materials Inc., 1997*

Language Expression: Paragraphs and Sentence Sequence

Directions: Read the paragraph. Look for the correct order for the sentences. Fill in the answer circle for your choice.

Sample

A. 1. Last summer my family took an exciting vacation.

2. While in New York we toured many museums and other places of interest.

3. We began the trip by flying from Los Angeles to New York City.

4. Just before coming home we went to the Statue of Liberty and the Empire State Building.

   (A) 1 - 2 - 3 - 4

   (B) 1 - 3 - 2 - 4

   (C) 3 - 2 - 4 - 1

   (D) 4 - 3 - 1 - 2

1. 1. First we saw how the potatoes are washed, peeled, and sliced.

2. Today our scout troop toured a factory where potato chips are made.

3. The last things we saw were the machines that package the chips.

4. Then we watched the sliced potatoes cook in vats of bubbling oil.

   (A) 1 - 3 - 4 - 2

   (B) 2 - 1 - 4 - 3

   (C) 2 - 4 - 1 - 3

   (D) 4 - 3 - 2 - 1

2. 1. Then the food was delivered to the car on a tray that hooked over the window.

2. People parked and a waiter or waitress came to take their order.

3. Today, however, we do not drive in—we drive through.

4. Drive-in restaurants used to be very popular.

   (F) 1 - 3 - 2 - 4

   (G) 2 - 1 - 4 - 3

   (H) 3 - 4 - 1 - 2

   (J) 4 - 2 - 1 - 3

Answers: A Ⓐ Ⓑ Ⓒ Ⓓ   1 Ⓐ Ⓑ Ⓒ Ⓓ   2 Ⓕ Ⓖ Ⓗ Ⓙ

Reprinted from TCM 2131, How to Prepare Your Students for Standardized Tests—Intermediate, *Teacher Created Materials Inc., 1997*

Math Concepts/Applications: Geometry and Measurement

Directions: Read each question and find the correct answer. Fill in the answer circle for your choice.

Samples

A. Which two lines appear to be parallel?

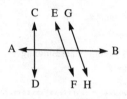

(A) AB and CD

(B) EF and GH

(C) CD and EF

(D) AB and GH

B. A living room is 6 meters wide and 8 meters long. What is the area of the room?

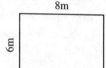

(F) 14 m

(G) 28 m

(H) 48 m

(J) 50 m

---

1. Which two figures are congruent?

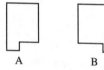

(A) A and C

(B) A and D

(C) B and C

(D) B and D

---

2. What is the volume of this cube?

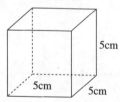

5cm

5cm   5cm

(F) 15m³

(G) 30m³

(H) 90m³

(J) 125m³

---

3. How long is the diameter of this circle?

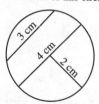

3 cm

4 cm

2 cm

(A) 2 cm

(B) 3 cm

(C) 4 cm

(D) 9 cm

GO→

- -

Answers: A Ⓐ Ⓑ Ⓒ Ⓓ   1 Ⓐ Ⓑ Ⓒ Ⓓ   2 Ⓕ Ⓖ Ⓗ Ⓙ   3 Ⓐ Ⓑ Ⓒ Ⓓ

B Ⓕ Ⓖ Ⓗ Ⓙ

Reprinted from TCM 2132, How to Prepare Your Middle School Students for Standardized Tests, *Teacher Created Materials, Inc., 1997*

Vocabulary: Multiple Meanings

Directions: Read the pair of sentences. Find the word that fits in both blanks. Mark the answer space for your choice.

Samples

A. He left a_____to let his mother know where he was going.

The musician hit a wrong_____.

(A) letter
(B) tone
(C) message
(D) note

B. The_____was closed for a week after the fire.

I hope I_____this test.

(F) road
(G) pass
(H) understand
(J) forest

---

1. They will_____the best person to do the job.

Her neck got stiff from sitting in a cold_____.

(A) hire
(B) draft
(C) find
(D) breeze

4. Many people are very influenced by their_____group.

We saw him_____down the street to find out if the bus was coming.

(F) age
(G) look
(H) peer
(J) income

---

2. She arranged a_____of peach blossoms in the vase.

He will_____the seeds with the hose.

(F) bouquet
(G) water
(H) branch
(J) spray

5. The young shepherd always_____the sheep.

He sometimes_____to overeat.

(A) wants
(B) tends
(C) minds
(D) inclines

---

3. "This road is so bumpy it will_____your bones," he said.

The jam is in that tall_____.

(A) shake
(B) rattle
(C) jar
(D) container

6. The pirates will_____them on that lonely island.

She has a new_____sweater.

(F) strands
(G) purple
(H) abandon
(J) maroon

Answers:
A Ⓐ Ⓑ Ⓒ Ⓓ   1 Ⓐ Ⓑ Ⓒ Ⓓ   3 Ⓐ Ⓑ Ⓒ Ⓓ   5 Ⓐ Ⓑ Ⓒ Ⓓ
B Ⓕ Ⓖ Ⓗ Ⓙ   2 Ⓕ Ⓖ Ⓗ Ⓙ   4 Ⓕ Ⓖ Ⓗ Ⓙ   6 Ⓕ Ⓖ Ⓗ Ⓙ

Language Expression: Grammar and Syntax

Directions: Read the words in each box. Then read each question below the box. Choose the best answers. Fill in the circles for your answer choices.

Samples

> I. Mr. Johnson is going to the football game.
> II. I am going to the football game.

A. Which of these words is used as an adjective in the sentences?
   (A) going
   (B) football
   (C) game
   (D) to

B. What is the subject of sentence I?
   (E) Mr. Johnson
   (F) is going
   (G) game
   (H) the football game

> I. Those bees have a hive in the maple tree.
> II. The bird has a nest in the maple tree.

1. Which word in these sentences is a preposition?
   (A) those
   (B) maple
   (C) in
   (D) the

2. What is the subject of sentence II?
   (E) a nest
   (F) bird has a nest
   (G) the maple tree
   (H) The bird

> I. The pencil is broken.
> II. The pencil was under your notebook.

3. Which of these words is used as a noun in the sentences?
   (A) notebook
   (B) under
   (C) the
   (D) broken

4. Which word in these sentences is a past tense verb?
   (E) was
   (F) is
   (G) under
   (H) broken

> I. The boys are at practice now.
> II. The boys were at practice on Friday.

5. Which word in these sentences is a present tense form of be?
   (A) were
   (B) at
   (C) are
   (D) on

6. Which of these words is used as an adverb in the sentences?
   (E) practice
   (F) were
   (G) now
   (H) Friday

GO→

Answers:
A (A) (B) (C) (D)   1 (A) (B) (C) (D)   3 (A) (B) (C) (D)   5 (A) (B) (C) (D)
B (E) (F) (G) (H)   2 (E) (F) (G) (H)   4 (E) (F) (G) (H)   6 (E) (F) (G) (H)

Reprinted from TCM 2132, How to Prepare Your Middle School Students for Standardized Tests, *Teacher Created Materials, Inc., 1997*

Use or Abuse?
Interpreting and Sharing
the Results

The Use and Abuse of Test Scores

Test scores have power; if misused, the power can damage a child or young person forever. Always remember that

- A low score can damage an already fragile self-concept.

- A grade level equivalent score is a guess. It does not mean much. It does not mean that a child is performing at that particular grade level. It should never be given to students or parents.

- One right or wrong answer can make a big difference in a score. That is correct—just one answer! Sometimes it means the difference of a few months, sometimes a greater difference.

- Unless otherwise stated in the technical manual, test makers expect students to have a grade level mastery of the English language.

- Knowledge of poor test scores can lower teacher and student expectations. It can crush enthusiasm and motivation for learning.

> **Unless otherwise stated in the technical manual, test makers expect students to have a grade level mastery of the English language.**

- More often than not, testing places the emphasis on competition rather than development of individual talent. As a result, product becomes more important than process. In a competitive environment, teaching has a tendency to become coaching for a test, and real learning and real thinking are crowded out (Neill & Medina, 1989).
- The professional judgment of the teacher, coupled with authentic measures, is a far better indicator of student achievement and potential than a standardized test. Placement decisions should rest with the teacher or multiple measures but never with a single standardized test score.
- Standardized testing, skill practice, and test-wiseness strategies should be integrated parts of the total curriculum, not taught as isolated subjects.
- Testing is a big business. It is "primarily controlled by commercial publishers and nonschool agencies that produce norm-referenced, multiple-choice instruments designed to rank students cheaply and efficiently. These instruments were initially created to make tracking and sorting of students more efficient; they are not intended to support or enhance instruction" (Hammond, 1991, p. 220).

Interpretation of Test Scores

It is important for the teacher to analyze the test; it is not wise to rely solely on descriptions provided in the manual. For example, the content validity portion of one test manual makes the statement that the reading portion of the test measures the *depth and breadth* of a student's word knowledge. What are depth and breadth? These terms don't tell why these particular words were chosen for this standardized test, their sources, or why they represent knowledge that should be mastered at certain grade levels.

> *"To provide reasonable interpretations of students' performances on standardized tests, the teachers must be very familiar with the actual test being administered. Teachers should be encouraged to obtain a copy of the test battery and carefully review the items. Only when the teachers know exactly what is asked of students can they possibly offer reasonable interpretations of the test" (Ansley, 1997, p. 278).*

Next, the teacher must analyze the score report for each student; scores for each subtest should be carefully reviewed. Individual subtest scores tell a much greater tale than an overall score for the entire battery. This is true because a high subtest score can be averaged with a low subtest score, resulting in a middle range

The professional judgment of the teacher, coupled with authentic measures, is a far better indicator of student achievement and potential than a standardized test.

overall score that can mask a students' lack of mastery in a particular subject area. For example, look at the score report below:

Amanda Rose: Grade Seven

Subtest	Stanine	Percentile	Grade Equivalent
Language Mechanics	7	83	8.4
Reading Comprehension	8	90	8.9
Mathematical Computations	3	21	3.4
Overall Battery	6	65	6.9

The overall score says Amanda is just a little below grade level. That is not an accurate or true picture of her ability. Rather, Amanda has strong skills in language and reading, but her math skills are poor. She needs intervention with math, a fact that might be overlooked if only the total score is reviewed.

Most importantly, the teacher should look at the number of items the student attempted and the number of those attempted that are correct.

The teacher should not look at just the grade equivalent scores or percentile rankings. Most importantly, the teacher should look at the number of items the student attempted and the number of those attempted that are correct. This is the *accuracy factor*; check back on page 22 to review this concept. Before a teacher proceeds in the test score analysis, it is imperative to know these two numbers for each subtest: raw score (number correct) and number attempted. Then, consideration should be given to plotting a relationship chart; such a chart is an excellent way to report scores to parents and students.

The following raw scores have been obtained by Johnny, a fifth grade student, on a standardized reading test:

Vocabulary   Raw Score 32 (number attempted: 34)

Comprehension   Raw Score 10 (number attempted: 10)

*The number possible in each section is 48.

Look at the two relationship charts below for Johnny. These charts plot Johnny's score two ways, first without the number attempted and second with the number attempted.

First, see what happens if the number attempted is not known. The chart that is plotted would look something like this:

Score Relationship—Chart One

VOCABULARY	COMPREHENSION
X	
***************** *****************	grade level average
X	# correct

X = grade equivalent for number correct

An interpretation at this point might indicate that Johnny has a serious reading comprehension problem.

Consider, though, the number attempted and the accuracy factor and plot it as a "what if" score, i.e., what if Johnny had correctly answered all he did? The picture changes dramatically:

Score Relationship—Chart Two

VOCABULARY	COMPREHENSION
X^y	
***************** *****************	grade level average
X	# correct

y = grade equivalent for number attempted
X = grade equivalent for number correct

Consider, though, the number attempted and the accuracy factor and plot it as a "what if" score, i.e., what if Johnny had gotten all he did correct?

Johnny's problem may just be one of rate; he reads slowly, but he is accurate in his comprehension. In fact, he got every question correct that he completed. Is he struggling to comprehend, or is there some other factor that is interfering? His word knowledge is good, so his potential to comprehend is excellent. Authentic assessment can help the teacher determine why Johnny is reading so slowly.

✔ Does he have a vision problem? Does he wear glasses? Did he wear them for the test?

✔ Does he lose his place? Does he make repeated regressions?

✔ Does his attention wander?

✔ Does he have difficulty making the transition from oral reading to silent reading?

✔ Is English his second language? If so, does he need extra time to translate?

This formula will work for any subtest:

Number right ÷ Number attempted = Accuracy Factor

Then the teacher can make interpretations. It is much more important, a much stronger foundation for interpretation, to know that a student got all or nearly all correct that he or she answered than to know **just** the number correct. A raw score is nearly meaningless unless the accuracy factor is known.

Score Profiles

If a standardized test is mandated by the district or state, it is normally scored by a professional testing service or, at the very least, the district level testing staff. Sometimes these reports contain the number of items a student attempted in each subtest, sometimes not. Teachers should be sure to find out whether or not this information is provided; if not, they should make note of the number attempted in each subtest for each student before the answer sheets are sent for scoring.

Typically, a score report for a standardized test battery will look something like the one on page 67. Categories will, of course, be different, depending on the subtests of the battery and the grade level for which it is intended. Each standardized test battery has unique scoring characteristics and reporting standards. The Iowa Test of Basic Skills, for example, reports a developmental standard score (SS) to report the student's academic development as it

> It is much more important, a much stronger foundation for interpretation, to know that a student got all or nearly all correct that he or she answered, than to know **just** the number correct.

Basic Skills Battery **Profile Report** **Student Information:**
Grade Level: 2

Subtests	Scores: SS	NS	NP	Percentile Rank Low 10 25	Average 40 60 75	High 90 99	Comments
Vocabulary	210	8	95			→	**Strength:** Reading scores are well above average.
Comprehension	180	7	89		→		
Total Reading	185	8	92			→	
Math Computation	177	6	60		→		**Weakness:** Math application skills
Math Application	160	5	39	→			
Total Mathematics	168	5	48	→			
Language Mechanics	172	5	58	→			
Language Expression	171	5	57	→			
Total Language	171	5	57	→			
Total Battery	174	6	66		→		Overall achievement is somewhat above average; this student scored better than 66% of second grade students nationally.

SS = Standard Score   **NS = National Stanine**   **NP = National Percentile**

relates to nationwide averages in grades four, eight, and eleven. The Nelson-Denny Reading Test norms require a doubling of the comprehension raw score before stanines and percentiles are computed. Other tests have their own quirks. Teachers should always read the interpretation guidelines that accompany a profile or narrative report. The rule here is beware and be wise!

Talking with Parents

A key element in assessment is involving parents in the process by reporting and communicating progress with them on a regular basis. Parents often ask questions such as the following:

> Why was my child tested?
> How did my child do?
> What do the scores mean?
> How did my child do in comparison to other students in the class?
> How will these scores be utilized?

Parents are partners in education and need to play a significant role in the determination of goals and expectations for their children. "By assessing parents' beliefs and communicating frequently, teachers can include parents in the most precious experience of their children's lives—their education" (McClay, 1996b, p. 70).

The teacher should let parents know the purpose of the testing. Tell the parents whether the test was locally, state, or nationally mandated. If applicable, let the parents know that the results will be used to evaluate and improve the school and district programs.

First, the teacher should be thoroughly prepared to explain the content of the standardized test and to correctly interpret the scoring profile. A score profile should never just be mailed home! When reporting test results to parents, the teacher should show them a relationship chart with number attempted and number correct. Then, it is imperative that the teacher help the parent interpret the meaning of these scores and chart a course of action if the child needs to build skill in one or more areas.

The teacher should prepare an achievement report that lists the positive aspects of a student's academic development. Avoid using grade equivalents and total battery scores. From the subtests of the standardized test battery, the best scores can be highlighted. Poorer scores can still be presented in a positive fashion.

A key element in assessment is involving parents in the process by reporting and communicating progress with them on a regular basis.

This isn't to say that the teacher should gloss over a problem area; rather, the teacher should take control of the problem and say, "This is what needs to be done!" In other words, teachers should identify strengths first, then identify areas where improvement is needed, and finally provide parents with concrete ideas for setting the student on a course of action to make the improvements.

Standardized scores should be presented to parents as part of an assessment package, never in isolation. Teachers should have many authentic assessment measures to either confirm the results of the test or provide evidence that the score is not valid. This will facilitate comparison of a student's accomplishments with his or her previous work, not the work of classmates; it will also help parents understand how the student learns and works. The teacher should be sure that parents understand that the standardized test is only one of many tools used to evaluate each child.

> **Standardized scores should be presented to parents as part of an assessment package, never in isolation.**

Finally, teachers should ensure that parents understand basic standardized scoring terms. These terms are discussed in the Basic Principles of Standardized Testing section of this guide, but a "parent friendly" explanation might look something like this:

Stanine: These can range from a low of one to a high of nine.

1, 2, or 3 =	Below Average This is an area that needs improvement.
4, 5 or 6 =	Average This represents about the same performance as others who took the test.
7, 8, or 9 =	Above Average This represents performance that is better in this area than others who took the test.

Percentile Score: This score gives a more detailed description of how a child compares with other students who took the test. If La'Tisha scored at the 74th percentile, she achieved a score as well or better than 74 percent of the other students who took the test. So, if 100 students took the test, La'Tisha scored better than 74 of them.

Talking with Students

Most important, teachers should praise students for the effort they put into giving their best performance on a standardized test. As soon as the test is finished, the teacher should encourage students to talk about the testing experience. Students can do a quick write, share a thought, or write a journal entry. It is important that the students be given an opportunity to talk about their frustrations so they don't allow negative feelings to grow. "Immediately after the test, encourage your students to talk about their experience. Discussions may help them to vent any frustration they feel about the testing process."

When score reports are ready to be distributed, set up individual, private conferences with students. It is important to share their strengths with them and focus on the positive: "Juan, you made great improvement in spelling. Good job!" "Jerry, you got every math problem you did correct!" The teacher should integrate score reporting with a strong basis of authentic assessment measures. "Authentic assessment values approximation; students have a sense of accomplishment for what they have learned rather than a sense of defeat because a product is not perfect" (McClay, 1996a, p. 65). Finally, the teacher should map out an individual plan with each student for areas that need improvement. Older students can be encouraged to interpret their own performances. Do they think the scores are accurate? "Be careful of the words you use. Students may have a natural curiosity or anxiety about test results; they could be easily misled by unguarded comments" (Bagin, 1989, p. 2).

At the risk of sounding redundant, never give a student a grade equivalent score. It can damage self-esteem; it can influence self-expectations; it can give an untrue picture of performance; it can destroy the motivation and desire to learn.

Support from the Administration

Standardized achievement tests "have become pawns in a political chess game. In most such states, these tests are transformed from evaluation devices to high stakes accountability tools. In many such situations the focus for these tests has shifted completely away from test score interpretations at the student level to interpretations at the school or city level. This is a large departure from the purpose for which these tests are constructed" (Ansley, 1997, p. 278).

Teachers must be student advocates and share with the administration their professional knowledge about the uses, limitations, abuses, and cautions associated with standardized testing. As Rotberg states, "We cannot improve our schools by giving more

> Teachers must be student advocates and share with the administration their professional knowledge about the uses, limitations, abuses, and cautions associated with standardized testing.

73

tests. The danger is that myths about testing will lead to policies that are irrelevant and counterproductive in addressing the nation's most pressing education problems" (1996, p. 35).

Concluding Remarks

Question number ten from *"Test Your Knowledge of Standardized Testing" (page 3)* was answered in this final chapter. It should be False; the most important piece of information in a standardized test is a subtest score, not an overall score. Subtest scores show strengths or weaknesses in mastery of a particular skill or subject area. Teachers should share reliable test information with parents and students, applauding individual achievement and effort while setting a prescribed course of action for skills that need improvement.

Teachers should use caution when interpreting and reporting results of standardized tests. Scores are often misused, and the results can be disastrous. Authentic assessment measures must hold equal weight in the student evaluation process; in fact, results of authentic assessment should take precedence over standardized test scores. "Assessment should hold the promise of improving teaching and learning in the nation's schools" (Lieberman, 1991, p. 219). Standardized testing should never have punitive consequences for students or for teachers.

> **Teachers should share reliable test information with parents and students, applauding individual achievement and effort while setting a prescribed course of action for skills that need improvement.**

✔ Students should never be labeled as a result of a standardized test score.

✔ Students should never be tracked as a result of a standardized test score.

> *In many ways, the misuse of basic skills tests has been most damaging to the very students the tests were especially intended to help. Many studies have found that students placed in the lowest tracks or in remedial programs are those most apt to experience instruction geared only to multiple-choice tests; such students work at a low cognitive level on test-oriented tasks that are profoundly disconnected from the skills they need to learn. Rarely are they given the opportunity to talk about what they know, to read real books, to write, or to construct and solve problems in mathematics, science, or other subjects. In short, they are denied the opportunity to develop the capacities they will need in the future, in large part because our tests are so firmly pointed at educational goals of the past (Hammond, 1991, p. 222).*

✔ The competence of a teacher should never be judged by the standardized scores of his or her students.

References

Ansley, T. (1997) The Role of Standardized Achievement Tests in Grades K-12. In G.D. Phye (Ed.), <u>Handbook of classroom assessment: Learning, achievement, and adjustment</u> (pp. 265–285). San Diego, CA: Academic Press.

Bagin, C.B. (1989). <u>Talking to your high school students about standardized tests.</u> (ERIC Digest No. 106). Washington, DC: ERIC Clearinghouse on Assessment and Evaluation. (ERIC Document Reproduction Service No. Ed 315435)

Hammond, L. D. (1991). The implications of testing policy for quality and equality. <u>Phi Delta Kappan,</u> 73(4), 220-225.

Hall, J.L. & Keline, P.F. (1991, April). <u>Preparing students to take standardized tests: Have we gone too far?</u> Paper presented at the annual meeting of the National Council on Measurement in Education, Chicago, IL.

Herber, H. L. (1993). <u>Teaching in the context areas.</u> Needham Heights, MA: Allyn & Bacon.

Hoyos, G. (1996). Help your students beat the testing game. <u>Instructor,</u> 105(5) 60–65.

Jasmine, Julia (1997). <u>How to prepare your students for standardized tests.</u> Westminster, CA: Teacher Created Materials, Inc.

Kraus, R. (1971). <u>Leo the late bloomer.</u> New York, NY: Simon and Schuster Books.

Lieberman, A. (1991). Accountability as a reform strategy. <u>Phi Delta Kappan, 73</u>(4), 219-220.

McClay, J.L. (1996a). <u>Learning centers.</u> Westminster, CA: Teacher Created Materials, Inc.

McClay, J.L. (1996b). <u>The multi-age classroom.</u> Westminster, CA: Teacher Created Materials, Inc.

Madaus, G. (1991). The effects of important tests on students: Implications for a national examination system. <u>Phi Delta Kappan, 73</u>(4), 226-231.

Manzo, A. (1997). <u>Content area literacy: Interactive teaching for active learning.</u> Upper Saddle River, NJ: Prentice Hall, Inc.

Mehrens, W. A. (1989). <u>Preparing students to take standardized achievement tests.</u> (ERIC Digest) Washington, DC: ERIC Clearinghouse on Assessment and Evaluation. (ERIC Document Reproduction Service No. ED 314427)

Meisels, S.J., Dorfman, A. & Steele, D. (1995). Equity and excellence in group-administered and performance-based assessments. In M. Nettles and A. Nettles (Eds.), Equity and excellence in educational testing and assessment (pp. 243-261). Norwell, MA: Kluwer Academic Publishers.

Neill, D.M., & Medina, N.J. (1989). Standardized testing: Harmful to educational health. Phi Delta Kappan, 70(9), 688–697.

Rotberg, I.C. (1996). Five myths about test score comparisons. The School Administrator, 54(5) 30-35.

Ruddell, M.R. (1997). Teaching content reading and writing (2nd ed). Needham Heights, MA: Allyn and Bacon.

Rudner, L.M. (1994). Questions to ask when evaluating tests. (ERIC/AE Digest) Washington, DC: ERIC Clearinghouse on Assessment and Evaluation. (ERIC Document Reproduction Service No. ED 385607).

Ryan, C.D. (1994). Authentic assessment. Westminster, CA: Teacher Created Materials, Inc.

Ryan, K. & Cooper, J.M. (1995). Those who can, teach (7th ed.). Boston, MA: Houghton Mifflin Company.

Salvia, J & Ysseldyke, J.E. (1991). Assessment (5th ed). Boston, MA: Houghton Mifflin Company.

Sanders, W.L. & Horn, S.P. (1995). Educational assessment reassessed: The usefulness of standardized and alternative measure of student achievement as indicators for the assessment of educational outcomes. Education Policy Analysis Archives, 3(6).

Shepard, L.A. (1991). Will national tests improve student learning? Phi Delta Kappan, 73(4), 232-238.

Stake, R. (1991). The teacher, standardized testing, and prospects of revolution. Phi Delta Kappan, 73 (4), 243-247

Weirsma, W. & Jurs, S. (1990). Educational measurement and testing (2nd ed.). Needham Heights, MA: Allyn and Bacon.

Wheeler, P. & Haertel, G. (1993). Preparing students for testing: Should we promote test wiseness? (EREAPA Publication Series No. 9301) Washington, DC: ERIC Clearinghouse on Assessment and Evaluation. (ERIC Document Reproduction Service no. Ed 374163.

Wigdor, A.K. and Garner, W.R., (Eds.)(1982). Ability testing: uses, consequences, and controversies. Washington, D.C.: National Academy Press.

Worthen, B. & Spandel, V. (1991). Putting the standardized test debate in perspective. Educational Leadership, 48(5), 65-69.